HAITI

The Aftershocks of Hope

"One American's Rude Awakening"

TrubuPRESS is a subsidiary of the Trubu Media Group whose interests include but are not limited to fiction and non fiction stories from the black experience throughout the American and African Diaspora.

Publisher: TrubuPRESS
Editor: Neo Blaqness
Cover Design: TrubuPRESS
Proofreaders: Cynthia Utley, Tamika Coleman

HAITI: The Aftershocks of Hope
Copyright © 2013 Yolantha Harrison-Pace

To order HAITI: The Aftershocks of Hope
visit http://trubupress.com
or call (872) 22TRUBU

Booksellers:
Retail discounts are available from TrubuPRESS. Inquiries about volume orders can be made via the phone number listed above.

ISBN-13: 978-0615816258
ISBN-10: 0615816258
Published by TrubuPRESS

PRINTED IN THE UNITED STATES

Dedication

To all the nobodies in the world...

*I'm just one of those nobodies
who somebody told
about a Somebody
that loves everybody
and doesn't want to
leave out anybody.
This book is written especially
for everybody who has ever felt
like a nobody
and wondered
if anybody cared.
I'm a living testimony
that Somebody does care
and has a Divine Plan
for everybody,
Even you.*

CONTENTS

TABLE OF CONTENTS

TABLE OF CONTENTS

TABLE OF CONTENTS

TABLE OF CONTENTS

TABLE OF CONTENTS

TABLE OF CONTENTS

TABLE OF CONTENTS

Foreword

I have an auntie who is no longer with us. One of her sayings, when she would visit someone with children was to ask "where are those little crumb snatchers?" Everyone would laugh and children would always come and give her a hug.

She was a well-meaning but crazy mouthy Christian woman- a real Bible Thumper but with a heart of pure gold. She died from years on her hands and knees inhaling chemicals working herself to the bone scrubbing people's floors while staying with a cruel husband.

There wasn't a "Saint" in her very Bible believing church who wasn't trying to get her to leave him- and that was something they never preached. But, in her case, the cruelty was just too inhumane– even for them.

But she prayed and she stayed until, finally, he could not take her endurance of spirit and he left. She and the children never had ever enough money for anything but, somehow, God always just led people to give.

She would spend a half day or more cleaning a house for relatively little money. As skinny as Popeye's girlfriend, Olive Oil, she would move furniture in each room and by the time she left you could eat off of every surface.

And she left Christian tracts everywhere– those little Bible lessons on bits of paper. She would stop the car and leave in phone booths. If she owed the doctor $500 and only had $5 she would mail it in cash and put a tract in every bill. I am sure she drove a lot of people crazy but nobody ever harassed her for money. I think they were too scared to call. They would have to hear at least 20 minutes about Jesus before they asked for their money.

When I was a boy, we all used to run away from her. But when I became a man, I realized that Jesus was the only reason she even survived. I found within myself a great love for her and her faith despite the fact that she could be so very annoying with it.

I thought of my auntie today as I completed the edit of Yolantha Harrison-Pace's new book HAITI: The Aftershocks of Hope. For the first time since losing my dear auntie, I have been utterly moved by the passionate obedience of a woman to the spirit of God within her.

I mercilessly wrestled with the edit of this book. How do you edit Paul at the Isle of Patmos, or Peter at Antioch, or Moses at Mount Sinai, or Jesus at Gethsemane? How do you measure the words of another's wilderness experience to determine the correctness of a walking and waking epiphany?

In my own book, *Epiphany,* I wrote *"If you work really hard, one of the best and most influential persons in life you will ever have the pleasure of meeting, will be the undiscovered you."*

After a myriad of renditions, redactions, and advice and concerns from well meaning professionals, I simply had to make the editorial decision to let Yolantha, be Yolantha– Raw, Real, and Uncut.

The book isn't just about Haiti and the tragic state of things there. It is really about the struggle of our spirits to recognize and heed the call above being comfortable or even correct in the eyes of others.

There are times where you will be both blessed and annoyed by Yolantha Harrison-Pace as she strives to walk the line between faith and futility trying to bring the literal and spiritual bread of life to those made accustomed to settling for crumbs.

Nevertheless I invite you to break bread with this book and be full in a way that you have never known before. Yolantha Harrison-Pace is not just one of my authors, she is an amazing work of God's art. She is The Potter's Rembrandt.

-Neo Blaqness, TrubuPRESS

Introduction

This book is not just about Haiti. It is about being called. It is about recognizing the call, answering the call, and fulfilling the call. This book is about my personal, intimate, relationship with God. It is about my struggle to hear God and to hear God clearly.

This book consists of excerpts from my conversations with God. I speak to God and God speaks to me just like I do with my family. At times, what I say to God may appear alarming or disrespectful. But I claim the promise that God is the same yesterday, today and tomorrow.

I claim the same infinite mercy, grace, and patience as God gave to King David, a man after His own heart; Rahab, the prostitute; Saul, who became Paul; Job, who was challenged by his friends to curse God; Martha, the busy body; Jacob, who refused to let go of an Angel 'til the Angel blessed him; Thomas, the ultimate doubter- to name just a Biblical few.

It is that same infinite mercy, grace, and patience that allows me to clarify, justify, question, whine, complain, and wrestle with the Angel of God. This book is my toast to a country that God blessed me with as testimonial ground– a country where I am often told by many of its people that I am the first African American they have known to ever set foot in their village or valley or mountainside.

The country? Haiti. Haiti, the land upon which God has honed, sharpened and deepened my relationship with Him. Thus, I raise my communion cup to the heavens and say "HERE'S TO HAITI: Kiss, America, Kiss!!!"

I wrote this book to share what I've experienced on the mission field. Me, a nobody, an every day little Negro girl raised on the wrong side of the tracks in Amarillo, Texas. Me, a food stamp, "gubment cheese" recipient. Me, a twice married victim of horrendous spousal abuse, who habitually tends to look for love in all the wrong places.

Me, who grew up with a huge stuttering speech impediment. Me, who grew up unpopular; could barely find anybody to go to prom with; ate lunch at the nerd table, and was always the last person picked for team sports. I still marvel daily that God, the creator of the entire universe, would choose and use me. And if God can use lil' ol' me, He can definitely use big ol' you.

I wrote this book, HAITI: The Aftershocks of Hope to inspire, encourage, and to call hearts into action on behalf of abandoned Haitian children I found living like wild animals and dying on the mountain sides. Barely two hours away from the blessed red, white and blue shores of my beloved homeland, my America.

The Back Story

"There you go again being controversial.
You're such a maverick."

L ooking back, I realize that this was a statement meant to control me, but, instead, it was the kindling that inspired a mere spark to become a flame. As a child, I remember the same words were used to describe Iva Matthews.

Iva was a huge, buxom, powerhouse in the local African American community of Champaign, Illinois where I grew up. When I was in the 8th grade, she was the boss of the radio waves every Sunday evening. Iva introduced me to the public arena by reading one of the first poems I'd ever written over the air.

Iva Matthews was notorious for doing good deeds. One of her most Godly deeds occurred every November when she spearheaded a gigantic Thanksgiving dinner for her "Honeys".

Her "Honeys"?

The homeless, America's castaways, America's tired, America's poor, America's refuse. Every Thanksgiving, Iva's "Honeys" came in huddled masses from miles around to be fed.

In addition, Iva loved children and was obsessed with providing supervised activities to keep them off of the streets. As a child, I loved being around her.

I remember thinking, "When I grow up, I want children to love being around me the same way I love being around Iva Matthews".

Controversial and a maverick- yes that was Iva Matthews. In spite of her wealth of goodness, Iva always seemed to be under attack. Growing up, I couldn't understand why a woman so saintly was constantly being picked on and ostracized or, as they use to say in the

Black churches, she was being "buked and scorned".

After I graduated high school, I visited Mrs. Matthews, who was, then, residing in an assisted living center. During my visit, I naively asked a question that had always been on my mind: "How come with all of the good that you do, folks are always picking on you?"

This huge woman, now in the advanced stages of myasthenia gravis, (what us kids used to call the elephant disease) laughed bellowing piano scales of glorious sounds through the air. Her arms, as thick as my torso, rippled with delight at my accidental rhyme.

Still embraced in the delight of her own laughter, she cocked her head toward me about half an inch. Her Volkswagen sized body wouldn't allow her to move much more. Then she whispered, "Baby, when I'm under attack, it's a sure fire indication that I'm doing the right thang. When you're working on the Lord's side, all hell breaks loose. When things are all smooth, quiet, and howdy-howdy, then the Devil ain't upset. Cause then, little darling, whose side are you really working on?"

The bulk of my life, I too have tried to do the "right thang". In the summer of 2007, God showed me 76 starving and abandoned children in a small village of Gade Hiram, Haiti. Children that He challenged me to feed, clothe, provide clean water, shelter and to educate.

When we began preparing for our next journey to Haiti, my daughter Erin, who had been traveling with me for two years, began confirming dates with the missionary organization that I'd traveled with for several years when she received an email:

February 11, 2008

Hello Erin,

Thanks for the email. These dates are firm. At this point I look for no change.

Due to the circumstances on our past trips, unfortunately, you and your mom can no longer travel to Haiti with me.

The forms that you all signed clearly state the rules and guidelines of [Organization Redacted]. By signing this, you agreed to abide by these rules. Erin, this is not old news, these are things your mom and I have discussed over the years. I have been lenient up to this point, but somewhere I have to take a stand. I believe in following the rules and guidelines for everyone's safety and benefit.

If you or your mom want to discuss this further, please let me know.

[Name Redacted]

We were devastated. Weeks were spent trying to clear our names, trying to find out why we had been banned from traveling with the organization to Haiti. Requests for copies of the signed guidelines that we had committed to were denied. Written accounts of the alleged infractions I had committed were requested and denied. Written documentation and information concerning discussions and behaviors requiring leniency were requested and denied.

However, in one phone conversation, reference was made to me having contacted some of the leaders of the Haitian community regarding 76 abandoned children that I had been introduced to during the summer of 2007.

Once again, I asked for documentation stating what guidelines or rules I had broken by my commitment to helping those children. No details were provided.

Finally, about 2 months later after a wretched night of tossing and turning, God said, "Peace. Be still. Let it go".

A Call to Christian Accountability

A few years back, my teenage daughter, Diamond, and I were talking about a friend of hers who was on the sensitive side and was getting teased unmercifully by some of his peers. I tried to have a little compassion for her friend, but my daughter responded, "No mom, he doesn't need any pity, he just needs to MAN UP!"

Later on that day I overheard two women talking. One was whining and complaining about an incident that had happened at work. Her coworker told her, "You better wipe your tears and hitch up your panty hose. Woman, you better MAN UP!"

These two incidents made me think about my Christian walk. And I challenged myself to stop putting off writing this book and to actively map out a speaking venue and to develop a fund raising campaign for the children of Haiti.

I told myself to stop whining and complaining and being so sensitive and making excuses. I challenged myself to grab my faith by the ovaries, pull up my big girl panties and "CHRIST UP!!!" .

Acknowledgements

Special shout-outs and gratitude go to: My father and mother, Raphael and Elaine Harrison. My father, who made it his job to provide me with a foundation for building a relationship with our Lord and Savior, Jesus Christ.

My mother, who got up early every Sunday morning and prepared five children for Sunday School, and got us stuffed into a 1959 Star Chief Pontiac to go learn about God.

Diamond Pace, my youngest daughter, whose delight and joy sets the standard, the quality, and zest for life that children deserve all over the world.

Erin Pace, my oldest daughter and missionary companion, whose calming, peaceful spirit helps to keep me grounded and accountable.

James and Artie Atkins, phenomenal African American leaders who acknowledged my talents and opened the door of encouragement that provided me, even as an adult, with an *I Can Do* spirit.

The late Pastor Willie Newby, who baptized my youngest daughter, Diamond, and planted the seeds encouraging me to personally study to show myself approved before God.

Pastor Tim Mathis, my current Pastor, who has watered the seeds planted by my spiritual mentors of the past. In addition, I thank him for his sermons that agitated my soul, and disturbed my comfort zones, and dared me to stand toe to toe with Matthew 28:19, 20- *The Great Commission*.

Attorney Jeffrey Dohrmann, Esquire, a blast from the past. One of my students who found me again and challenged me to get off the runway and stop living my life in a holding pattern waiting for someone else to determine when I should fly. Thanks for bringing me

ACKNOWLEDGEMENTS

back to my authentic, quintessential God created self.

Iva Matthews. Thank you Iva for showing me as a little girl, who grew up on the wrong side of the tracks, the power of a woman.

Eddie Arnold, for the initial invitation to "come go with me to Haiti".

E is for the Eternal light of Jesus

D is for the Divine appointment of God

D is for Daring to question the status quo

I is for Inspiration to go the extra mile

E is for Enough not ever being Enough for the good of God

Eddie, for that moment in time, one of my heroes.

And a final shout out to the scripture Romans 8:28- *All things to work together for good to those who love God, to those who are called according to His purpose.*

HAITI

The Aftershocks of Hope
"One American's Rude Awakening"

Yolantha Harrison-Pace

———————

TRUBU PRESS
A Blood Legacy Publishing Company

"Doesn't anyone carry a handkerchief anymore?"

CHAPTER ONE
EARTHQUAKE?

From America I watched
The baby was caked in soot
People in a panic hopped over it without a second look
A new born fallen fresh from its mother's core
The mother crushed beside it half in, half out the door
For three days the baby pitifully cried
For three days folks ignored and stepped aside
It took three full days- then the baby died.

Somebody wipe the baby off! Please…just wipe the baby's eyes. Use a little spit and your thumb, or the corner of your apron like grandmother did. Get something…a rag…use your shirt tail. Doesn't anyone carry a handkerchief anymore?

Stop talking about them like that. Stop showing them as if they are aliens, sub humans…less than us. There's a mother running with her child.

"Run mother run! Run child run!"

Turn off the camera, that's not supposed to be shown. Is that a leg? Just a leg?

I rushed into my busy, busy office. Not again Jesus, no, not again. Wasn't September 11th bad enough? Wasn't Katrina Hurricane enough?

I chomped my spreading behind down. I was too far angry to acknowledge the groan of my wicker vanity chair. I wrapped my

CHAPTER ONE

flabby arms tightly around my chest and rocked and rocked and rocked like an insane person.

See that's what happens when they don't listen. Nobody would listen to me. But they're listening now. They hear me now. They see me now. They smell me now. They taste me now.

Nobody can hide now what I've been telling them all along. 'Cause they need to know what I know. But now it's gone, gone as it will never be known again.

However...I've got it. Right here in my over stuffed office, my den of hibernation with pieces of me everywhere. African masks... mammy candles...Aunt Jemima cookie jars...books by black after black after black authors, sprinkled with Poe, Shakespeare, Coulter, and Bible book after Bible book after Bible book, cuddled up next to my eclectic taste in fashion- my creative ruins.

Ruins. Port-au-Prince is lying in ruins. I will not cry. I will not give the gasping world all tuned into CNN the satisfaction. Cry as you must Haiti, but don't you let the cameras see.

Come here with me Haiti, find refuge with me in my office. This sorrow is too deep to share. Haiti, my disassembled, disemboweled, destroyed Haiti. Forever changed.

My arms hang heavy beside me. Petrified. This is enormous. What can I do? For ten years on the mission field God has taught me that He uses people to accomplish His tasks to fulfill His promises, to work His miracles.

But this is so very, very colossal. I've got to do something. Something huge. Something bigger than big. I'm afraid. I'm... afraid. Afraid of...of...disappointing God. But even worse. I'm afraid of ...disappointing Haiti.

CHAPTER TWO

THE DAY THE EARTH STUTTERED

Nobody listens to me. From as far back as I can remember as a child with a severe stuttering problem I was told, "Shut up! Come back when you have something to say!"

I am of the era when grownups believed that children were to be seen and not heard, let alone a stu-stu-stuttering child. I conditioned myself to be silent all through Hilltop Elementary School, Carey Busey Elementary School, Jefferson Jr. High School, Centennial High School, and most of college.

"Come back when you have something to say!"

I fixed that. I fixed that. I started writing things down. Folks began to listen.

Now the earth has stuttered. And nobody understands like I understand. They have got Haiti all wrong. But don't you worry Haiti. I'll fix you Haiti the way I fixed me.

Not that you NEED fixing, just like I didn't NEED fixing. I wrote me down. Now it's your turn. I am writing you down. Now the world will know.

See I love you Haiti because you always love me back. I believe that when you are in love, you tell everybody. So I'm telling everybody.

"I know, I know, I know....
How do you eat an elephant?"

CHAPTER THREE
NOBODY KNOWS

I lay on the couch with my head covered. I cannot watch, yet I'm compelled, drawn like an addict. I am fixed on the devastation. My skin is alive with the wretchedness. I itch all over with sorrow. I can't watch, but I'm so addicted to my love that I force myself to close my discerning eyes and listen... just listen.

I lay in a fetal position on the couch...a wimp. Not knowing where to start, how to begin. Yes, I know, I know, I know...how do you eat an elephant? One bite at a time. But I've never met an elephant eater. I've never even met a person who knew someone who was an elephant eater.

Sure, I know all about mustard seed faith. I've even used and experienced it. Yet, I hide under the covers, snorting CNN. Then God sends an angel who whispers, "The mustard seed is only a starting point." Then the angel asks, "Which do you want, Yolantha, an apricot seed or an avocado seed?"

Thus begins the fight of my life. My life seems to hinge upon the life or death of Haiti. What is my obsession? What can I do for you Haiti? My only weapons are my memories suit cased away in my secret journals. Snap thoughts of my time with you. Snap thoughts on the mountains. Snap thoughts of remote villages and valleys and pathways, places and challenges, men, women and children few African Americans have seen.

Secret thoughts, secret moments. Secret because some of it is so intimate, I dare not break face and reveal to anyone- my innermost me. Secret reflections of me embraced in my own spider webs, locks

CHAPTER THREE

and chains. My own personal strait jackets of inadequacies. My Haitian affair. The goodest of the good, the baddest of the bad, the ugliest of the ugly, the extra ordinary of the ordinary.

Nobody Knows The Haiti I've Seen

Fog thicker than carnival cotton candy
Spiders bigger than a grown man's hands
A naked boy riding a donkey with
A basket full of roosters perfectly
Balanced on his head
A street full of boys standing in line to
Get their heads dry shaved with a
Straight edged razor
Dogs so emaciated that they would be
Intimidated by a New York rat
A little baby in a bucket getting
A bath by his beloved 5 year old brother
Stars at midnight
On the mountains
Hanging so low
Pregnant with joy
Begging
To fall in my pocket
Nobody knows the Haiti I've seen.

*"Each angel kissed Jesus
goodbye on His forehead"*

CHAPTER FOUR
ANGELS

The angels came
from heavens around
Stirred by the horrible
rumbling of the ground
They all stood at attention
shoulder to shoulder
Watching the earth
as it began to smolder
They righted their halos
and fluffed their wings
They packed Mercy and Grace
and miracles to bring
This wouldn't get fixed
with just any bag of tricks
Or some fancy science
or new fangled arithmetic
Then it happened…
An avalanche of sobs,
Mountains of screams,
Monsoons of tears
As the ground shifted,
buildings fell,
Unleashing oceans of fears.
Each angel kissed Jesus goodbye
on His forehead
Scarred from the crown of thorns

CHAPTER FOUR

Each getting his and her assignment
As harps sounded
and Gabriel blew his horn
Raphael opened heavens gate
and out each angel flew
Zooming quickly to Haiti
they had much work to do
Holding children's hands
and consoling mother's lips
As breath after breath
inched away
sip by sip
Big strong men of muscles
and wise weaklings too
The angels rocked
and stood guard,
laid down beside them
to see them through
The anguish
The pain,
The dark,
The dust,
The confusion,
As life slipped away
and Port-au-Prince
became an illusion
The angels became blood splattered,
ragged and torn
Halos were bent,
their robes dingy and worn
They squeezed in,
walked through walls,

ANGELS

held heads in their laps
Soothed dying souls
in whose arms they were wrapped
Some of the injured
held on tight,
Being brave
And took longer
to die than others
Calling on God,
Some chanting voodoo
But all
calling for their mothers.
The angels soothed tongues
and wiped brows
And sometimes for days
they would just sit
It was a difficult job,
but somebody had to do it.
Over a million Angels
now assigned
for a lifetime to a place
Where generations of people
became an extinct race
Assigned to a country
that even before the quake
Needed untold help
and mercy
for pity's sake
So the angels all the better
for wear and tear
Persistently wait,
hovering in the rubble

CHAPTER FOUR

over there
Patiently they wait
standing guard over a land
Waiting to see
what we will do
Us
Made in God-Allah-Buddha image,
Called MAN.
So listen,
listen loud,
pa-rump-a-pump-pum.
I hear the drumming
Hang on Angels,
don't you fret
I'm coming.

CHAPTER FIVE
PROMISES, PROMISES

I t- the earthquake, happened on January 12, 2010. Fifteen days later, January 27th, it was unheard of. Rescuers pulled a girl out from under the rubble. Alive. Twenty-eight days later, February 10th another person, a man, pulled out of the rubble. Alive. A testimony of God's empowerment of the Haitian human will to survive.

What could that girl have been thinking for fifteen days? What tribulations that man must have faced for twenty-eight dark and painful days. Trapped. Alone. So what have I to be afraid of? Are my fears like the rubble of Haiti? Can I too, through God's empowerment of my human will, hold on tight and wait to be rescued through my fears?

Right here in the rubble of my office. Waiting, rather, procrastinating. Ten years worth of fears captured in writing. Scribblings stuffed full of poetic anxieties and transparent ranting, ravings, and prayers all entangled in the keeping of two promises.

PROMISE ONE: My promise to answer God's call that was to take me to *first time* places, *first time* people, *first time* happenings, *first time* causes, choices, reasons, *first time* first times.

PROMISE TWO: God will never ever leave me or forsake me. That in itself should be enough to unearth the rubble of my fears, if only I knew how to believe it. Can I, Yolantha, believe like that little girl, like that man? They are modern day proof that God will keep His promises. Can I keep mine?

Chapter Five

I know my faith is strong enough, but now with the earthquake are my expectations high enough. I have faith that God can heal me, but do I expect Him to?

Before it was just about me and God. All I had to do was to keep my promise of *going*. This earthquake has ruptured my promise. Calling for me to re-examine it. Just my going and having gone is now not enough. I have to tell others. Please don't ask me to do that God. It's all so personal.

CHAPTER SIX
JUST BLUE BOOKS

In 2000, I committed to be in it for the long haul. With blind faith, I believed that God was with me. In 2010, I'm still in it for the long haul. "God are YOU still with me?" How dare I doubt God? More like, God is asking, "Yolantha are you still with ME?"

God, I'm not sleeping very well. I keep waking up at two in the morning. I keep running away from all of the TV coverage. But it's my only link.

I keep escaping back into my cave of an office to hide. My office, where my stacks of papers even have stacks, I mindlessly shift one stack on top of another stack. I tie a bright yellow kerchief on my head, trying to feel better wearing my favorite color. It doesn't help.

For the fifth time, again, I pick them up. They're just blue books. Like the kind you take tests on in college. I like them on the mission field because I can fold them up and slide them in my bra.

Blue books full of my conversations with God. These treasured scrawlings are my documentation of my intimate, relationship with God. When I hear God, (the operative word is "when") I hear God clearly.

Within the sacred covers of these thin blue books are my exams. They are my responses to my daily spiritual quizzes and my documentation of living the test. These blue books are prompts based on my breath, my steps, my choices, my actions concerning my call to Haiti. But on the surface, they are just blue books.

CHAPTER SIX

Here's one still tightly folded and stuck together with missionary sweat. No longer sky blue. But murky, antiqued by my own body fluids, like day old snow.

I inhale the sweat stained cover trying to smell the smell of Haiti. In slow motion I meticulously unfold it, careful not to rip it, for fear of ripping a hole in my soul.

It's one of my first, from ten years ago. I wrote in pencil then. The pages are wavy. I tilt the faded number two pencil lead closer to my office lamp. I remember this. The fragile page says…LEAVING AMERICA.

CHAPTER SEVEN
LEAVING AMERICA

Are we there yet?

PLOP! Luggage appeared beside me. I was sitting at Burger King in the crowded Miami Airport. The curly brown haired owner, seemingly a college kid, dropped his luggage, turned and walked away.

"What the-hey?" My head muttered. "Too close for comfort!" My skin shouted.

Basic, primal, non-missionary language marched to the edge of my tongue. This missionary thing was not going to be as easy as it seemed.

Second non-missionary thought…that litany of words heard since September 11 in every airport about reporting suspicious behavior and not letting any one tamper with our luggage or give us any suspicious items.

Third non-missionary thought. I digressed and became even more secular. Third non-missionary thought…espionage movies, 007, Get Smart, Mission Impossible…the ol' luggage switch-a-roo… the bomb in the briefcase scenarios…a bu-bu-bu-bomb???!!!

"LORD HEP ME JESUS!!!" Finally a thought worthy of missionary consideration.

The young stranger bopped up, placed a tray on our table, hunkered down, and began to eat. We both ate in silence, except, one of us was chewing and swallowing awfully loudly. I think it was me.

Something pinched my right thigh, a buzzing, burning sensation, like an ant bite. I scratched, trying not to disturb our silence. I thought a bug or something had crawled up my pant leg because I didn't own a cell phone. I scratched harder.

"What is stinging me?" I prayed I had not spoken out loud. I dug into my pocket. It was something metallic and warm. I giggled. I had forgotten about the 10 little silver pocket crosses that I'd purchased at my hometown Christian book store in Danville.

I had purchased them with the brilliant notion of using them as witnessing tools on the mission field in Haiti. Something inside of me said, "The mission field is here and begins now." I tripped over my tongue as obedience stared me down.

I freed one of the silver crosses from my pocket. Taking a deep breath, I betrayed our silence. "How far are you going? Are you traveling alone? Can I give you this?" I didn't wait for any response as I slid a cross over the table. I continued to ramble, still not pausing for an answer, "If you don't want it perhaps you can pass it on to someone else who might need it!"

The object seemed to vibrate in the Burger King light. The stranger picked it up and stared at it for a long, long time. He leaned toward me. He whispered, "I'm going on my first missionary trip and I'm scared."

I had an uncontrollable urge to wrestle him to the ground and tickle his fears away, like my brothers used to do to one another when one of them was scared or having a very rough day. I just nodded. I sat and listened to him and his anxiety concerning the language barriers, and whether someone would be there to meet him and would he be able to do a good job? I watched him gulp his last bite. He glanced at his watch, and then grabbed his luggage, "Gotta go!"

"God bless you." I said leaning forward, my eyes locked on to his American baby blues. "You'll do fine", assured. He walked away rubbing the cross between his thumb and fingers. One cross down, nine to go.

LEAVING AMERICA

I was on the mission field and I hadn't even left America yet. I hadn't said much, just listened. It was my first missionary lesson. The Great Commission 101. The best missionary tool a missionary may ever possess is the tool of listening.

"You'll do just fine," I whispered to and for myself. Words of comfort and encouragement we all long to hear. All of my life, all I ever wanted was to be loved. To feel validated. To have others feel, that I am worthy. To have someone think about me, be concerned about me, take an active interest in my well-being as I simultaneously think about and take an active interest in them.

That's every man, woman and child's desire, no matter their race, creed religion, color, economics or gender. In this, I know I am not unique.

"Ya wanna come to Haiti with me? "

CHAPTER EIGHT
AND WHAT DID YOUR HUSBAND SAY. . .

All of my life I wanted to please God. But it seemed like I was failing miserably. I was in my second marriage. I was bound and determined to get it right, but it was going all wrong. Mothers and guardian mothers don't seem to teach their daughters the truth of marrying a man who will love you the way that he loves the church. The key truth we have forsaken; if a man neglects the church he will neglect his family.

I thought if only I could get him in a church to his liking, everything would then be "howdy-howdy, glory-glory, spiffy-keeno-groovy". This was my criteria:

ONE: A church that taught the Bible, both the Old and the New Testament. My daughters must know the difference between Moses and Noah, Daniel and Sampson, Miriam and Mary.

TWO: A Pastor who could bury men and my family.

THREE: A Pastor who could comfort me in the event that I had to bury a loved one.

FOUR: A Pastor who could comfort my loved ones in the event they had to bury me.

FIVE: A Church with "in-reach" taking care of her own flock.

SIX: A Church with "community outreach" serving the neighborhood.

SEVEN: A Church with "global outreach" ministering over and beyond the red, white and blue shores of America.

CHAPTER EIGHT

So I church hopped until I found two that were to my liking and that might be to my husband's liking. I took him worship shopping and he picked "The White One" as it was often referred to so not to be mistaken for, "The Black One" of the same name.

It was a gorgeous churchy church with high angelic vaulted ceilings. A church lavishly embellished with a stained glass Jesus holding a stain glassed little lamb whose eyes followed you no matter where you sat in the sanctuary.

The walls were flanked with traditional Christian emblems standing at attention. A majestic steepled edifice adorned with unobtrusive screens for modernized videos proclaiming the Word. There were conservatively camouflaged speakers with invisible face mikes, the latest in techno-savvy for proclaiming "Thus saith the Lord."

And for any who might be in doubt every pew had a bird's eye view of a table that fascinated me even as a child. The table that without shame testified, THIS DO IN REMEMBRANCE OF ME.

The day we joined, I was accosted by a tall distinguished looking member of the church who said, "Ya wanna come to Haiti with me? We have our next meeting on Thursday."

My immediate response was "Yes!!!" The man stumbled back utterly shocked at my seemingly spur of the moment response.

"You pray about it," he stammered. "I already have." I beamed.

CRITERIA NUMBER SEVEN: A church with global outreach.

Ecstatic, I looked around to high-five my husband. In all of my excitement I had not noticed that he had slipped out of the sanctuary. I found him waiting for me in the car.

Before I could even get the car door closed I bubbled, "God called me to go to Haiti and be a missionary. You have got to go with me. Oh I'm so nervous, this is beyond, beyond. Just imagine you and me serving God together!"

"God called you, he didn't call me." It wouldn't have hurt so badly if he would have followed that statement with, "But you'll do just fine."

My bubble exploded with his gunning of the engine. In silence we drove home. My husband never stepped foot into church with me again. I painstakingly learned if he didn't love the church, how could he love me?

Perhaps that's why I'm addicted to Haiti. I love Haiti, and Haiti loves me back. Haiti tells me thank you, we appreciate you, we miss you, when are you coming back, we can't wait to see you.

Haiti brings me papayas, and oranges and pineapples. Haiti looks me eye to eye and says, "Hurry back!" Haiti gathers a crowd as we all walk to Church.

"What do you want to be when you grow up?" I asked the boy.
"A person," he replied.

CHAPTER NINE
WAITING

The little navy, burgundy black, Haitian boy percolated with joy; proud to practice his English. It startled me. Didn't the little boy's parents teach him not to talk to strangers? Noses pressed to the huge window we both stood waiting to board the final plane for Port-au-Prince, Haiti.

Good ol' privileged American me. I looked at my watch. I got into the habit of wearing men's watches for their sturdiness, compared to a delicate woman's watch. The little Haitian boy, breathing his little breath on me arched his back, leaned on his tiptoes as he too peered at my watch. He stared hypnotized by the large tick-tocking contraption.

"Hi," I said.

"Halloo," his teeth overtook his head. My heart fell into his grin.

"What do you want to be when you grow up?" I asked the boy with my most sugary sweet Kentucky southern belle charm.

"A person," he replied.

Very amused, the Americanisms ingrained in me would not let me resist, I asked, "Well what will you be as a person?"

His dark eyes squinted at me with the weight of a heavy thinker. I thought perhaps he was searching and measuring his mind for just the right English words.

"What will I be as a person?" His intonations mimicked mine perfectly. "A GOOD person," he proudly answered.

I threw my head back delighted with laughter. He stared at me seriously, like a boy-man. I am truly in love and I'm not even there yet.

CHAPTER NINE

I learned later that the infant mortality rate in Haiti is so very high that the young boy had every right to brag about having lived to be seven years old. With his peers dying all around him he would consider it an accomplishment to live long enough to grow up and become a "person".

Yet how noble of him, that if he became privileged enough to grow up, he wanted to be good at it. What about me? I had thirty nine years on the little boy. I asked myself, how good was I at being a person?

CHAPTER TEN
GIGGLING

BOOM-BOOM, BOOM-BOOM

I knew everybody on the plane, including the pilot, could hear my heart beating. It was reminiscent of the Edgar Allan Poe story, The Tell Tale Heart.

Lover's Embrace

YES!!!
The window seat.
I clumsily tumbled in
after blocking traffic
and boinking the person
standing behind me
repeatedly in the chest
with my backpack
full of crackers
and crayons
and
Vacation Bible School cut-outs.
Sorry
I mouthed to the passenger behind me
Wheeeeeeew,
I expelled air
I fell into my window seat clutching my Bible
Wondering why I had been holding my breath.

Something caught my attention
flittering from my Bible then
It landed on my sleeve.
It was a tiny ray of sunshine
It danced through my window
as if it had bounced
off of a heavenly prism.
Did anyone else have one?
I inventoried the surrounding travelers.
Nope.
Only me.
"Do you love me, Yolantha?"
Who said that?
Who here knew me
and could call me by name?
I slumped in my seat,
kept my head still
eyeballed left
and eyeballed right
I noticed I wasn't breathing again
and my mouth was just doing its own thing.
It choked out "yes…but…"
"Then feed my lambs."
Pained, my eyes crinkled shut.
Again,
"Yolantha, do you love me?"
I could just barely nod my head.
"Feed my sheep"
I didn't dare breathe
for I remembered my Bible
just enough to know that there
was a third time coming.

GIGGLING

He whispered my name
"Yolantha."
"YES!!!"
I answered loudly
before God could ask me again.
"What?"
asked the person
squeezed next to me on the airplane.
"Sssssssorry."
I stuttered.

Who giggled? It was the sound of miniature wind chimes. People were still standing in the aisle waiting to claim their seats. Others who had found their placements were embraced by headphones or were deeply buried in novels and newspapers.

The man way across at the other window seat had his mouth open like a train tunnel and a spit drop was clinging to his chin. He was asleep and the plane had not even left the runway.

There it was again, somebody was giggling at me. Was it an Angel? Oh God, please don't tell me that now I'm hearing angels. What have I gotten myself into?

Frantic I looked up the word Angel in my concordance. My hands were shaking. A--A--S, no that's too far. A--M--now flip a few pages to the right.

Panic pinched my nose constricting the air like when I was a child in Sunday School competing in a Bible drill. A sweat drop scurried a path down from my left armpit.

Andrew, one of the twelve disciples? Andronicus, a relative of Paul? Paul? Paul the road to Damascus? Paul, who used to be Saul? My mind still stuttering for an answer.

CHAPTER TEN

I couldn't breathe. Where was my air? Where was the stewardess? Was this what folks called a panic attack? Was I gonna die all alone on this airplane before I even set foot in Haiti?

"Shhhhhhh…"

Was that an Angel of God?

"My Son, Jesus, will walk with you and He will embrace you arm in arm with a lover's embrace. So go, walk confidently, speak boldly making disciples in all the nations baptizing them into the name of the Father and of the Son and of the Holy Spirit, and then teach these new disciples to obey all the commands I have given you; AND BE SURE OF THIS my daughter- that I am with you always even to the end of the world."

The voice had emphasized, "AND BE SURE OF THIS". I quickly thumbed through my Bible and by George there it was in red ink. There was the phrase. Exactly as Jesus had spoken it. "AND BE SURE OF THIS that I am with you always even to the end of the world." The same promise, "I WILL NEVER LEAVE OR FORSAKE YOU!"

The Bible flipped itself to the front without my help. ANGEL!!!

"There it is," I exclaimed.

I must have spoken out loud. My seat partner looked annoyingly at me over her glasses. Oh no, I think I'm gonna cry. Not me, not four brothers and the only girl, me.

My nose burned with the stale smell of breathing in other folk's air. Sitting on the airplane for the first time as a a a mih mih mih Missionary.

For a whole year I couldn't even say it out loud. The word was too sacred for the multitude of sins that I had committed in the first forty five years of my life.

I wanted to scramble off of the plane. The aisle was packed with last minute people boarding. People who moved with assuredness, determination, and acted like this was normal. No escape. My seat partner was evidently more comfortable now because she was taking up more than her share of our seat.

Squished up against the window seat, my flesh side was hyperventilating and screaming, "LET ME OFF, LET ME OFF, PLEASE LET ME OFF I CAN'T BREATHE!!!".

I looked at the people around me to be sure I had not shouted out loud. I frantically stuffed 4 sticks of Wrigley chewing gum into my mouth and searched for the upchuck bag. The airplane was vibrating and rolling. The front of the plane tilted and lurched like the start of a carnival ride.

"Kerchunk!"

The wheels went up into the belly of the plane

"Oooooooooooooooooooo Jeeeezuz!!!"

"I'm here," the voice said, "I'm here".

The Awkward Moment

I heard someone breathing.
I sure hoped it was me.
It's too late to turn back now.
I'm in the air
Over the awesome Atlantic
totally in God's hands.
My thoughts as I knew them ceased.
My walk as I knew it ceased.
I am too ignorant to have an agenda.
My guarantees,
My birthrights as an American ceased.
I must do God's will on their turf.
"Toto, you're not in Kansas anymore."
Oh no.
God quoting the Wizard of Oz?
This time I knew it was me giggling.
Quickly I looked down
at my Wal-Mart combat boots.
I heard someone breathing.
I sure hoped it was me.

CHAPTER ELEVEN
PORT-AU-PRINCE

Inhale-Exhale

I inhaled deeply
of my color
My eyes melted
into a comfort zone
I'd never felt
in my life
I watched them
Not watching me
A freedom
I never felt before
In my America
I watch them
Purposefully
watching me
In toleration
of my existence
I exhaled fully
and all of me
Was still
all of me.

Crowded

I brushed up against
The paint of my skin
Kissing the paint
of their skin
They were me
I was them
And our spirits agreed
No hostility
No subtext
No hidden agendas
The bliss
of my heart
reached out
Embracing
the blood
of my blood

PORT-AU-PRINCE

The Smell

The smell"
A thin yet familiar voice
startled me
"Oh it's so strong.
I can taste them"
I looked
at my fellow
white female
Missionaries
Huddled
tightly together
Posse'd up for protection
They looked
like I have felt
All of my life
in America
"Stay together,
we only move as a group,"
Our strong white team leader barked.
I smiled
my tight lipped
Americanesqued smile.
"Yes Kemo Sabe"
I thought in my best of
Tonto and the Lone Ranger
childhood memories.

CHAPTER ELEVEN

No You Don't

My bladder called. I, just out of my freedom as an American, and out of forty five plus years of habit, began to stride toward the bathroom. I had taken five steps and felt the familiar American stares. Mercy overtook me. I walked the five steps back toward my female companions of fear.

"I'm going to the bathroom," I announced. "Does anyone else need to come?"

"YES", in unison.

SWOOSH!! The other missionary women latched onto me. I wanted to cry for the me in them until one piped up and announced loudly, "NOW I KNOW HOW YOU FEEL."

Mercy left me.

"No you don't, you have no clue."

I prayed deeply that I hadn't spoken that thought out loud.

PORT-AU-PRINCE

The Capital

Maybe it was all
displaced pride and respect
and a Pavlovian response,
But I had no problem
seeing Port-au-Prince
as the Haitian
Washington, DC.
But at the same time I felt
Like I was in an Indiana Jones movie
or had fallen into the pages
of a National Geographic Magazine.
Still ,in the midst of my
unfamiliarity
I felt so familiar.
"Beep, beeeeeep, beeeeeeep!!!"
Nader the taxi driver honked
as he whipped us from the big airport
to the small airport.
I closed my eyes
"Beep, beeeeeeeep, beeeeep!!!
Honk, hoooonk!!!"
I was in downtown New York City.
"Beep, beeeeeeeep, beeeeep!!!
Honk, hoooonk!!!"
I opened my eyes,
I was in Port-au-Prince.

"Beep, beeeeeeeep, beeeeep!!!
Honk, hoooonk!!!"
I closed my eyes.
I was in downtown Chicago.
"Beep, beeeeeeeep, beeeeep!!!
Honk, hoooonk!!!"
I opened my eyes,
I was in Chocolate City DC,
I mean
I was in Port-au-Prince.
There were street vendors
like outside the grocery stores
in the Hispanic section
of Houston and Chinatown
Chicago and LA.
It was so very, very, very
Harlemesque beautiful.
"Mistah, Mistah, gimme one dollah,"
shouted a man at our taxi.
I closed my eyes.
I was on the streets of San Francisco.
"Hey mister, ya wanna buy a watch"
I opened my eyes.
And I embraced
Port-au-Prince.

Oh Yes The Smell

Oh yes the smell
The delicious
eau-de-cologne
The aroma
of a people
Not afraid
To smell
like
People

"Come ooooooon airplane, you can do it!!"

Chapter Twelve
I'M REALLY HERE

Flap Your Arms

Run real fast Yolantha,
flap your arms, flap your arms!!!
The flight from Port-au-Prince to the airport in Pignon
Is forty minutes
in a small Run-Real-Fast-
Fred-Flintstone-Prehistoric-Sky-King-
Bubble-Gum-Cracker-Jack-Prize
Airplane.
My body begins to think on its own.
I scrunch up.
My shoulders involuntarily reach for my ears.
My elbows start moving as if they were wings.
Come oooooon airplane, you can do it!!
I look at all of us well fed missionaries,
Hoping they are flapping too.
The other missionaries seemed to be
just nonchalantly looking out of the windows;
not in the least bit paying attention.
Not one ounce of concern.
Like a child, I lift my feet,
An old superstition I once heard my country cousins say.
"If you lift your feet as the plane
starts moving down the run way,
It made the airplane lighter for take off."

Shooooot in this tiny thang?
I'm gonna try any tactic to help
get us fat missionaries off the ground.
Since none of the other missionaries are on point,
I'm gonna have to do a whole lotta flappin'
And the pilot, look at the pilot.
I'm not suppose to be able to see the pilot from my seat.
And he's got his window rolled down
and his elbow stuck out the window.
Oh no, the pilot puts on some mirror sunshades,
then cops a lean like a teenager
doing drivebys in the inner-city.
He starts the plane.
The roar is so loud my body
became one with the engine
like it does at a rock concert.
A huge puff of air entered my mouth.
I gagged, the taste of diesel fuel.
Without any fanfare he took off
like he was Johnny Travolta
riding a Harley.

Where's The Runway?

Where's the runway? Where's the runway? Where's the runwaaaaaaaaaaaaaaaaaaaaay??? I almost lost it. I lifted my feet again. I hope it works for landing too.

All I could recite was the 23rd Psalms. The Lord is my Shepherd I shall not want. He maketh me to lie down in green pastures. I didn't realize that God meant that literally.

Over 2000 years after Christ, mega years after the Psalm was written by King David, God made our plane to lie down in the green mountain pastures of Haiti.

"Breathe, Yolantha Breathe."

My eyes peered through the window. Children were everywhere. I'm really here. I'm really in Haiti.

The pilot dumped us, looked at his watch and then donned his Travolta mirror sunglasses. I swear, he gunned the airplane engine, then he did a U-turn, and he gunned the engine again and took off straight up in the air without even taxiing. My heart skipped a beat.

"America?" my heart said, like a child calling after his mama.

"If you can't say anything nice..."

CHAPTER THIRTEEN
THE ZACHEUS EXPERIENCE

We were missionary movie stars. Children were grouped all along the fence by the field where we landed. They watched us and posed for our cameras. They were hungry to see what the plane was bringing them today. My pockets were full of starlight mints and "cheeclay" as the children called it-gum.

There was one little boy, punier than the rest, standing away from the other children. His posture expressed that he was unimpressed by the "blancs". He just stared off away from us at a distance. The other children scurried with the enthusiasm of chipmunks gleaning their precious rations of missionary mints, missionary gum and missionary hugs.

"Blanc" which technically translates as "white" is what all non-Haitians are called, including me, in spite of the chocolate hues of my skin. But my one friend didn't seem at all interested in our missionary love offerings. I strode boldly toward him, unwrapped a stick of gum and placed it at his lips. Like a baby bird, he dutifully opened his mouth, accepted the gum still avoiding eye contact.

"Jesus I'm hot!" announced one of my fellow missionary mates.

"Well no duh," I thought, turning away from my new friend, then prayed to God I hadn't responded out loud. "We are closer to the equator here than in Kentucky," Once again I prayed to God that I had not spoken out loud.

I rejoined the other missionaries. A river of sweat poured down my back. I was beyond annoyed at all of the whining and complaining I had endured from my fellow citizens. I was learning first hand the definition of ugly Americans- our arrogance, our impatience, our sense of entitlement, our egos, our inalienable right to freedom of speech which of course includes whining and complaining and lest I forget, loud boisterous laughter.

I thought I was a very docile and tolerant person but I almost pimp-slapped one of us at the crowded Port-au-Prince airport when one of my fellow Americans announced, "Oh how they smell."

Another of us responded loudly, "They don't use deodorant in 3rd world countries. Here tap on some perfume- there that's better."

I stepped over a little and tried to blend in with the aromatically beautiful Haitian crowd around me.

"It's soooo hot. Aren't you hot Yolantha?" Again the complaint of the air conditioned privileged was registered. "You make me hot just looking at you."

I wear all of my clothes on missionary trips. Enough clothes for 10 days. This allows much more room for food and Vacation Bible School supplies in my luggage. My mission fashion statement always caused the other missionaries to look at me as if I was crazy.

"Aren't you hot with all of that on?" whined one of my compatriots.

I heard my grandmother, "If you can't say anything nice, then don't say anything at all."

So I chose not to respond.

My grandmother was a cotton picker in the deepest south of Texas. She always wore a t-shirt and a long sleeved man's shirt to pick cotton. She taught me an old slave tradition- if you wanted to stay cool, dress in layers. The layer closest to your body will become drenched with sweat and keep your body cool. I chose silence over sharing this tidbit of slave trivia knowing all of the extracurricular explanations that this line of conversation would birth.

You'd be amazed how many of God's tools (crayons, pencils, Bible crafts, matchbox cars, erasers, granola bars, and crackers) you can get into a suitcase if you opt to wear all of your clothes.

I also knew the discomfort was well worth the end result of feeding and educating children in need. I didn't want to appear judgmental of the other missionaries and the way they packed, so again, I opted to remain silent.

Our extreme heat sensitivity compelled all us missionaries to herd under the only lone tree at our makeshift airport. There we stood sucking up its meager shade. The Haitian children humbly stood in their sun, letting us missionaries bask in the shadow of their tree.

Smiling at the children smiling at me, for many, their first African American female missionary. I noticed that my little boy was no longer in sight. A leaf floated to the ground. I looked up. My expressionless friend, poker faced, smacking on his gum, had climbed the tree. He only wore a shirt so he leaned forward in a feeble attempt to hide his nakedness.

He stared down at me, his childness imprisoned in his blank stare of hopelessness. Was I losing my touch? Never had I been in the presence of a child for more than 15 minutes that I couldn't evoke a smile. So at fifty years of age, I hiked up my three skirts and climbed the tree.

My silent friend was shocked. He burst into a gigantic smile that swallowed his eyes and captured his face. His eyes popped open when I landed beside him. Shocked, he swallowed his gum. Out of sheer impulse, I whacked him on his back. The gum reappeared.

The other missionaries froze in mid conversation. I grinned like the Cheshire Cat of Alice in Wonderland and said to my fellow Americans, "Y'all are gonna help me down aren't you?"

In pure American male fashion one of the men responded, "You got up there on your own, you're on your own to get down." They all laughed.

CHAPTER THIRTEEN

I had a dilemma. The New Testament story of Zacchaeus and the sycamore tree rushed to the front of my brain. I remembered the song we used to sing in Sunday School as children.

"Zacchaeus was a wee little man and a wee little man was he. He climbed into a sycamore tree for the Lord he wanted to see. Then as Jesus passed by his way, Jesus did say- Zacchaeus you come down from there, cause I'm going to your house today. For I'm going to your house today."

Sniggling and giggling my new friend and I sat perched in the tree eyeing one another. With a swift rustling of leaves, my new buddy jumped to the ground. He lifted his bony emaciated arms toward me, offering to assist me down. With the grace of a donkey, I let him help me, doing my utmost not to squish him.

Safely back on mother earth, my would be knight in shining armor squatted at my feet, in a protective watch, chewing his gum, grinning from ear to ear.

We waited for the trucks to arrive and carry us missionaries on up the mountain. I prayed briefly, "Oh God, Zacchaeus wanted so desperately to see Jesus that he climbed a sycamore tree. When your Son saw, Zacchaeus' determination, He called the man down and spent time visiting with him. A visit that changed the man's life. Oh God…I am humbled by this challenge."

What will be the outcome of my visit? I saw the dust in the far off distance. The trucks were coming. "later God, Amen…"

"I'm so hungry."

I couldn't believe that came out of one of the missionary's mouth. My secular side raised up again I felt like grabbing the missionary by the earlobe. I looked at overly healthy us, then at the bloated tummies, ribbed upper torsos, and pipe cleaner arms of the children crowed around us like statuesque trophies of emaciation as they stood in the sun sucking on missionary starlight mints.

THE ZACHEUS EXPERIENCE

I looked at the obesity of our missionary team, spraddled around the tree breathing hard, fanning with our huge plantation straw hats in the shade. I took 3 steps and stood in the sun with the children and began to hum...Zacchaeus was a wee little man and a wee little man was he, he climbed into a sycamore tree for the Lord he wanted to see, for the Lord he wanted to seeeeeeeeeee.

Missionary transportation:
Anything that will get you there.

CHAPTER FOURTEEN
TRUCKS

Rough Riders

"How far?" asked one of the missionaries. We all turned and looked at François, our translator extraordinaire, who had been waiting for us at the airport. Lanky, thin, with sparkly eyes full of merriment, a man we would call in Texas a long tall drink of water.

"12 miles missus."

Easy breezy piece of cake. I can handle this. twelve miles to the missionary compound. Fifteen minutes more and it will be official, I will be the "M" word. Let the God games begin. But...but...but... where's the road?

A dust storm skidded in upon us. As the dust settled...Three objects appeared. If wheels could walk, three sets of four eighteen wheelers, rancid with the smell of diesel fuel, inch wormed up next to us and parked themselves.

My eyes bugged out of my head like a frog. Surely I was in a Transformer Movie. Three mix-matched trucks with multiple car parts? Was that an eighteen wheeler front grill? Bailing twine? A chocolate brown extension cord?

I tried to focus on just one, and I use the term loosely. A black hood. A Pontiac hood ornament. One red door. two blue doors. One white door. No bumper.

SHA-WHOOSH a guy landed like superman, feet first out of the passenger window. A Major League baseball cap. An American football t-shirt and khakis. Four teenagers with the pizzazz of the Three Musketeers hopped off of the bed of the truck and approached us.

They walked with the grace of Fred Astaire and the swagger of Lil' Wayne. I was thrilled. My lily white counterparts were aghast. Each lad was dressed in khakis and an array of American sports team shirts and caps. Way to represent America, way to represent.

They began organizing our luggage and supply bins. I tried not to alter my normal blinking pattern. A game I had long since mastered thanks to my brothers. I inhaled a dashboard prayer. Thanks God for my brothers and the multitude of hours spent playing that notorious game of "made you flinch" then WHAM, you got punched in the arm for blinking.

I morphed into my poker face. A strategy which came in very handy for the vast number of things that would eventually bombard my sight and compete for my blink.

From inside another truck, a dark brown arm, darker than the brown in any crayon box I had ever seen pointed in my direction. He leaned his woolen head out of the window, with teeth whiter than dental porcelain and smiling like a river boat king.

"You will ride wit me, missus," announced my transformer limo -truck driver.

CHAPTER FIFTEEN
WELCOME MADAM

The Haitian truck driver proudly invited me over to this hodge-podge Piccasso-esque contraption. He reached outside of his missing window pressed the handle and let himself out of his truck. Striding majestically around and bowing like the best of French butlers, he extravagantly opened the red passenger door of this black bohemian artwork on wheels.

The young boys quickly worked and had now expertly layered the bed of my truck with our missionary belongings. As I approached the front seat, I was confused. More missionary supplies. There was no where to sit.

He pointed to the roof of his truck. I inhaled sharply, (but I didn't blink). The truck smelled of aged leather, tarnished silver with a hint of citrus. He grabbed my left elbow to steady me and like a chef expertly handling a choice piece of meat, he firmly planted my left foot on the edge of the supply laden frayed front seat. With a quick navigation under my armpits, then a boost to my behind, before I could say jack sprat could eat no fat he landed me onto the very top of the cab.

Nobody in America was going to believe this. Oh my goodness. Perched up high like this reminded me of my first beauty pageant parade as Miss Columbia College which led into a Miss Missouri parade and the myriad of 4th of July Parades- a portion of my life never shared or talked about. Have I come full circle?

I felt a full fledged guffaw coming on. I couldn't help myself. My hand automatically cupped itself in the position as I gave my best

Miss America wave at the other missionaries stoically arranged in the bed of the two remaining "transformer" trucks. All clinging white knuckled and perched precariously on top of containers of rice, beans and American missionary edible foods. There were tools and building supplies and solar panel stuff.

The exuberant truck driver leaned his pearly whites out of his window, beamed up at me, perched like a queen on her caravan throne.

"WELCOME MADAM! The childrun are hahpee dat you cuhm. Dey will be sooooo hahpee to see you. You bring duh childrun hope".

I smiled my most royal smile and nodded thanks like the Queen of England.

"What are you doing," asked my colored, Negro, Black, African American self?

Cringing with a guilty
Catholic-like conscience
In spite of my deep rooted
Southern Baptist-ness,
Somewhere from down deep
in my baby toe
came the prayer
"Forgive me Lord
for so many times I have sinned.
I must not get distracted.
I am here to do Your bidding.
To feed Your sheep.
What ever it takes
By any means necessary
That is my obsession
Nothing must get in my way."

WELCOME MADAM

Putting on my best
Miss America face
Majestically riding
atop of the cab of the truck
Full of food and supplies
and…and…and…
Hope?
It's on God, it's on…
Bring it!

With a jolt, I began the ride of a life time. The roads were so horrendous the twelve mile ride took over two hours to accomplish. Two hours which began my spiritual inventory.

"I must ignite a nation with an epidemic of hope."

Chapter Sixteen
OBSESSED

Why am I really here? I've lived the underdog--last one picked, overlooked, dismissed as a hopeless cause. It's the worst feeling in the world. Especially when you know you have something to offer. How do you know? Because God says so. And it's always been to His say so that I have clung prompted by three obsessions.

OBSESSION ONE: No matter what anyone says: I am made in God's image.

OBSESSION TWO: I can do all things through Christ who strengthens me.

OBSESSION THREE: All things work to the good for those who love the Lord and are called according to His purposes.

All things, not just Sunday things, not just a few things, not just a one time deal. This is not an entitlement based on race, gender, socio-economics or place of worship.

Therein lies my drive, my strength, my obsessions, my staying power, my hope. An obsession that cloaks me, a mantle I wear, a super cape I wear as I lift chins of the downtrodden, as I rock the unrockable, as I hug the unhuggable, and as I kiss the unkissable. I must ignite a nation with an epidemic of hope.

"Beat my heart beat
Walk the 12 miles
In my bare feet."

CHAPTER SEVENTEEN
FIRST IMPRESSIONS

Reflections

People gather
Along the briar spine needled fences posed as
Painted statues of poverty
As our motorcade drives past
Children move in slow motion
In the equatorial heat
Their ample lips hang loosely
Their eyes gaze like the elderly
In the nursing homes of America
Who have resigned to a life
They have no control over
The children's emaciated hopelessness
Reflects like old folkness
What an amazing American mirror I see

Children by Any Other Name

Haitian children were everywhere,
Peeking through bushes,
Running in packs down the road
Haitian children
walking backwards leading us
To some unknown where
Haitian children skipping along behind us
Protecting us by closing up the ranks
Haitian children walking hand in hand beside us
Welcoming us with
Eyes of wonder and joy
Everywhere I looked,
Haiti's children,
The consequences of political fall out
Yet children by any other name
are still children just the same.

Oodles and Oodles

I saw oodles and oodles of naked children
Staring with enormous cricket eyes
Tight pregnant bellies full of hunger
Their spirits spoke to me
"Beat my heart beat
Walk the 12 miles
In my bare feet"
I had no Americanisms
No points of reference
No encyclopedia, almanac or thesaurus
To define,
Explain or communicate
What I saw or…
What I felt.

"AMERICA… my heart said,
like a child calling after his mama."

GOD SHED HIS GRACE ON THEE

My Behind

My behind was riding in my brain
My arms were attached to my ears
I was experiencing
Extreme queasiness because of
Mainlining carbon monoxide
straight up my nose
From the trucks, our Haitian limos
That fumigated us with the smell of pure unadulterated,
Unpasteurized, unhomogenized
Diesel fuel from the trucks that jarred us up the mountain.
I pressed the back of my hand to my nose,
To smell my flesh
To find familiarity
Innnnnnnnhale
Exxxxxxxxhale,
Innnnnnnnhale
It didn't help.
It's been 2 hours to just go 12 miles
From the small wanna-be pasture of an airplane runway
To the missionary compound where we would stay
My behind was riding in my brain.

CHAPTER EIGHTEEN

We Stopped

Quick grab. Don't roll off. The truck sidled up to a long peach painted cement barricade. Out steps a black armed GI Joe. He ceremoniously halts us, like a carica-ture of the little green plastic army men my brother and I played with as kids. Like in an Indiana Jones espionage movie, he motions us in.

Surely my eyes deceive me…this does not compute. The time warp stood before me. I had just spent 2 hours, driving through utter devastation, abject poverty and human deterioration and now, as if in a Cinderella fairy tale or in a slice of Narnia, I'm surrounded by an upper middle class colonial styled American plantation. The porch or veranda if you will is adorned by 4 women, a couple of teenaged girls and a younger boy and girl, all dressed in various shades of white or dingy peach.

A motley crew I soon came to recognize as our…for lack of a better phrase and shadowed by my limited grasp of history, there standing before me was our…quote-unquote…"colored help." The house overseer, the cooks, and the laundry girls. A slice of America that I had never lived, but that I instantly recognized from my Coloni-al American history. However, it didn't seem to bother anyone but me.

The other missionaries were tut-tutting and pat-patting and right kissing and left kissing, smiling, whewing and fanning as they ex-changed "master/slave" pleasantries and entered our quote-unquote plantation home. My African American soul became like the fur on a cat's back that was being brushed the wrong direction. Naaaaaahhhhhh. Surely not. Say it isn't so as I deliberately unloaded my own gear off of the back of my truck. While the quote-unquote "hired help" joyfully unloaded the rest. "America?" my heart said, like a child calling after his mama.

CHAPTER EIGHTEEN

America The Beautiful

I unpacked
My meager belongings on the bed.
Meager belongings that reflected my inadequateness
I'm so ill equipped
No truth be told
I'm scared
Frightened
Feeling real raw and tender.
I reminded myself that
I came from a long line of community activists
Leaders, movers and shakers, uncloseted Christians.
But that ancestral breed is dying out.
I'm the only one in my lineage carrying the torch…
I mustn't fail
I can't fail
I can't let the torch burn out and even more so
I mustn't drop the fire.
It felt like tomorrow, next month and
The next year of God was depending on me.
I know God will forgive my shortcomings, but will Haiti?
I sat in the middle of the little prison like bed
Surrounded by my
American familiarities
With both hands over my face
Sucking in deeply the smell of me
I began to feel a little better from the nauseating

GOD SHED HIS GRACE ON THEE

Physically assaulting truck ride
I fingered my Wal-mart blouses and Goodwill skirts
Proof that amongst all of the strangeness
"I do exist"
My vulnerability prompted me to think of my daughters,
Erin and Diamond
I could feel the cry coming on,
my legs began to fold on the bed into a fetal position
NO
I took deep loud breaths to distract my tears
Oh God I'm scared
Tears,
NO!!! BACK I SAY, BACK!!!
YOU ARE NOT ALLOWED!
What would your brothers say
"Ya big cry baby!"
I found myself whisper-humming
"hmmmmmmm, hum-hummmm, hum hum hum hum
For purple mountains majesties, above the fruited plains…
Aaaaaaameeeeeerika, aaaaaameeeeerika…
GOD SHED HIS GRACE ON THEEE
AND CROWN THY GOOD
WITH BROTHER HOOOOOOOD
…and crown thy good with brotherhooood
…and crown thy good…with brotherhood
A huge alligator tear bleeds onto my Wal-mart blouse.
"I'm here" the voice says
Oh Jeez
snot starts to roll,
did I remember to bring Kleenex?
I had no clue what to do or how to be.
So I did something my Mother would have,

CHAPTER EIGHTEEN

let's just say, greatly chastised for.
Something Mother told me never to do.
I wiped my snotty nose on my sleeve
and I jumped up and down on the bed,
AAAAAMMMMMMMMMMMMEEEERICA,
AAAAAAAAAAAAAAMEEERICA
GOD SHED HIS GRACE ON THEEEEEE!!!

CHAPTER NINETEEN
SECOND IMPRESSIONS

Screaming Like a White Girl

That first night
Drifting in and out of rest
I breathed the children's eyes
Everywhere
My ears tasted the sounds of
The Creolic Spanish and French mixtures
Seasoned with the children's universal
Hot peppered echoes
Of laugher.
Exhausted beyond words
I cascaded into a deep, deep sleep.
My soul splashed against the shore,
The night ocean spat me onto the smooth sand
I stomped and stumbled and then shook.
Morning already?
Lost in space, I sat straight up
My body froze as icicles of pain
Overtook every inch of me
"this ain't my bedroom."
A tide of remembrance swept over me
The word Haiti echoed between the heartbeat
Tide of soreness from yesterday's truck ride
The hair on my skin prickled
I felt the eyes of yesterday's children upon me.

CHAPTER NINETEEN

I was being watched.

I moved my legs over the edge of the bed

They screamed begging for disobedience

I willed my sore body to peer out of the window

Nobody was there.

I limped across the room,

trying to figure what part of my aching buttocks to favor

Peered over the balcony..

Nobody.

My bruises got captured into the moment.

Somebody was looking at me.

Catlike, I sprang into the room,

yesterday's truck ride forgotten

Dropped quickly to my knees

Looked under the bed and proclaimed,

"PEEK-A-BOOOOOOO-I SEE-YOUUUUUUUU!"

Nobody.

Hmmmmmm, those eyes,

I couldn't shake the feeling of being watched.

I put Crest on my toothbrush and dry brushed my teeth

Conserving my precious flask

of missionary approved drinking water

Those eyes were still watching me

Following my every move.

I peered over at my things sitting on a little table.

The eyes were coming from that direction

Perhaps a child was hiding on the other side.

I tiptoed over to my make-up bag,

Sitting next to a bag of red twizzlers

and a can of planters peanuts

Which were flanked by

A chocolate chip cookie

SCREAMING LIKE A WHITE GIRL

My comb

My brush

A chocolate chip cookie?

I zeroed in on the cookie.

A chocolate chip cookie?

Peering at me?

My information rolodex went into immediate play.

It stopped under "N" for National Geographic

Then slowly flipped through one alphabet at a time

A-B-C-D-E-F-G-H-I-J-K-L-M-N-O-P-Q-R-S...TILL

It arrived at the letter "T" and hesitated as if waiting for me

To understand

Then it flipped back to the letter "A"

TATA? TATA?

TA-TA-TA-TAAAAAAA-RANTULA!!

In an octave I didn't even know I owned

I let our the most sissified

Academy-award-winning-

white-girl-running-from-the-monster-

done-tripped-and-fell-down-horror-movie-scream

The chocolate chipped cookie stretched forth its legs

As amazed I'm sure as I was,

Too petrified to run or jump

or what ever it is that tarantulas do.

The other missionaries ran in at my alarm

One pulled off his shiny new American sandal and

WHACK!!!

Stunned the chocolate chip spider cookie

and kicked it from the room.

I was so upset.

Not at the spider

But at myself...

CHAPTER NINETEEN

…for screaming like that.

All I could visualize was my 4 brothers, laughing

"Ya big sissy!"

Perhaps I shall leave this little 8 legged detail out.

No way could I live this story down

when I got back to America.

Chapter Twenty
BACK TO AMERICA

Control

Relinquishing control
Not an easy American thing to do
raised on John Wayne, Batman,
Bionic woman, Zorro and the Lone Ranger.
Relinquishing control.
Not an easy African American thing to do.
Raised on Rosa Parks, Malcolm X,
George Washington Carver and The Barack Obama.
Relinquishing control
Not an easy Christian thing to do.
After all I was raised on…on…on…
Well anyway God you never said anything about tarantulas.
Lions, giants and wolves in sheep clothing?
Yes…
But not one scripture on
tarantulas.

CHAPTER TWENTY

Tarantulas God? Tarantulas? This is not what I signed on for. Yellow fever, malaria, mosquitoes, bad water, food issues--that I signed on for--but tarantulas, come oooooooon-God?

Fingering the grayed edges of these first journals I'm amused at how irate I got with God. Why did I get so upset? As I think back, I was in control of the malaria, yellow fever and mosquitoes. I took all of my shots to prevent those diseases and I religiously saturated my self with the strongest of mosquito repellent throughout the day I could control what I ate and the water I drank Yes, control. An inalienable American right. Control. But I couldn't control when I might happen upon a spider.

The airplane ride home back to America is always hard. The only thing that brings me back is my daughters, Erin and Diamond. Or perhaps I would never ever return. On that ride home I am always a prisoner to the thoughts surrounding my missionary experiences. But dear François, my beloved friend, translator, caretaker and Haitian mentor explained "Haiti needs you in America. Otherwise, in just a short time you would be just another one of us. There is nothing here, in my country, to sustain you. From America you bring the children hope. Hope that no matter what--we will be able to make it." His words made me jealous. If only America could do that for me. Bring me opportunity, renewal and hope. All of my life I was cloned to believe that opportunity is what you make it, hope is what you make it, renewal is what you make it. Perhaps I've grown calloused, hardened, overly righteous, stiff necked. Perhaps I've grown --ungrateful. Because in America--I seem to always just miss--being able to make it.

BACK IN AMERICA

I gaze at my sweat stained pages and all of the scratches and scribbles of my journal entries. This book is suppose to be about Haiti. I've got the inside scoop that CNN is not showing, that CNN hasn't a clue about, that no media in the world is showing. News reports the supposed facts and statistics very rarely does it ever report the spirit, grace, enthusiasm, love, hope, joy and spirit of the people. The world must know about Haiti, but I keep coming back to me. Something I wasn't prepared for. A question crawls from beneath my skin. Is it easier to help and heal Haiti, than it is to help and heal me? The abuse, the neglect, the alienation, the bullying, being ostracized and humored, being tolerated…instead of celebrated? The very things that make me such a compassionate and effective worker in Haiti, are the very things I protect, I hide. My face stings as I remember my book coach, Martha Tucker slapping tough love words of encouragement as she read snippets of this book.

"Who are you? Who is Yolantha. If you can't write about you, then you will never be able to write about Haiti. Who ARE you? You're not real. You're not believable. If your reader cannot relate to you, then they will never read on, they will never turn the page."

For two days I did not slumber or eat. I wanted to just put down my pencil, shut off my computer, abandon this endeavor. But the eyes of Haiti's children haunt me and it's not at night. I usually sleep very well in spite of all I've witnessed in this devastated country. It's in the daytime. That's when Haiti consumes me. Can I not write about Haiti without explaining me? I took my dilemma to another critic. The woman had given me her card a few days earlier and had invited me to Panera's in order to get me involved in her virtual greeting card business. After we exchanged genteel conversation and sipped in southern fashion big tall glasses of exotic teas, I asked, "What is the key to a great salesperson?"

"Connection," she said without hesitation. If you, Yolantha, don't connect with your audience, then you, Yolantha, don't exist.

Even from the very first moment when you walk in a room, without any connection, then you, Yolantha aren't real. We will choose not to see you. People only acknowledge what they have in common. Then they are willing to listen. They might even help you feed the starving children or give to your cause."

Slice, slice, slice the knife cut deep into the hidden domain of my heart, the dungeon of my hidden secrets, the vulnerable parapets of my soul.

Here is my monstrous conflict. Am I Haiti? Is Haiti me? Is America's lack of having points of reference for me, the same kinship I share with America's lack of having points of reference for Haiti? Is that why the children of Haiti and I see eye to eye? To say I'm not believable is to deny every breath I have taken and will ever take. Is that what we have done to Haiti? The reality of Haiti's strife and pain is so extraordinary that we deny her existence? I was so angry my first trip back to America. How could we allow this to happen? I fumed. How can we witness the continuation of such poverty? How can we look the other way? How can we in the depths of our authentic souls look the other way?

My truth then becomes, how did I let this happen? How can my heart be so impoverished? How can my husband look the other way? The inside scoop on Haiti relies on me sharing the inside scoop about me. Now I weep.

MOMMY'S HOME!!!

"**M**omeeeeeee, Momeeeeeee, Mommy's home!!!" My daughters gather under my wings. "Did you miss me?" Of course they did. They were too young not to. On my first journey to Haiti they were only 15 and 6.

Upon my returns from Haiti there is a tightness behind my touch. Tears needing to be shed. But I fear the depth of my tears would traumatize my daughters so I keep them to myself. I hug my daughters just a few seconds too long. They catch me staring at them because after trips to Haiti I forget to look away, no-no-no, let's be honest, I don't forget, I CHOOSE to let my gaze linger. I picture them on the mountains of Haiti, jaundiced with yellow fever, stomachs bloated, and bodies teeming with gangrene, eyes staring off in a never land distance.

My umbilical cord of love yearns for my husband. He avoids me. Never asking of my wellbeing, never welcoming my return, never asking about my journey. Never in 10 years. So for 6 months, from July to January, there is a piece of me that is angry. Angry at America. Angry at my husband. Then joy comes again each year in February as I plan my return to a land that needs as much love as I do.

That's why I can't shake this earthquake. I am Haiti. The earthquake has shaken the innermost population of me. The central place where I abide. To help Haiti…helps me.

"We all recognized that scream."

CHAPTER TWENTY ONE

BUT WHY?

The missionary moved her suitcase and screamed
The male missionary ran in the room to the rescue
Boot in hand, poised and ready
We all recognized that scream
WHACK!!!
He missed
WHACK...WHACK...WHACK!!!
The tarantula was stunned but not dead.
WHACK-WHACK-WHACK-WHACK-WHACK!!!
"There I got him!"
The culprit was pulverized.
A little Haitian girl of 8
had followed the male missionary into the room
She looked at the tarantula
and then at the missionary and his huge boot
Then back at the tarantula
With tears streaming down her face
"But why?" she sobbed.
I was stunned,
none of us Americans knew what to say.

*"God wants me to see this
Through your Haitian eyes."*

THE HOSPITAL IN PIGNON

Culture Shock

The game plan:
God wants me to see this
Through your Haitian eyes…
Show me what you are seeing
Tell me what you are saying
Touch me what you are feeling
Feed me what you are tasting
Sing me what you are hearing
With your Haitian permission
Help me to understand

The Hospital

The babies lay open
Exposed
Like unwrapped chickens
In the supermarket meat section
Under mosquito netting
With feasting gnats
Fat from the running sores
Of babies laying open
Exposed
Like unwrapped children
In the hospital meat section
Under mosquito netting
With feasting gnats
Fat from the running sores
Once a day a nurse child comes in
It is time to turn the meat
So the gnats can eat
From both sides of the children
At the hospital in Pignon where
The babies lay exposed
With open sores
Their eyes begging to die.

The Duel

Looking at me, looking at him
His inevitable Haitian death,
My inevitable American life
We both stared boldly at one another
Hopelessness versus potential
Standing toe to toe
The baby's last breath, slaps me in the face
The gauntlet is thrown, the duel is on.

Baby Don

The baby lay
Big headed
Covered with a net
A net that had captured
A happy, happy Haitian fly
It happily buzzed and buzzed
The baby lay with his legs spread wide
His abdomen
Barely two inches high off the bed
Ribs protruding tightly
Each one countable
Big wonderless eyes
Mouth open
The baby made a sound
A dry cry
Too weak to breathe
Hoping air would fall in
And the fly
Happy, happy fly buzzed.
The fly doesn't have to wait on the baby to die
To have it's turn
It drops into the baby's open mouth
That waits patiently for air to fall in.

A few days later when I returned to visit the child he was gone. Praise the Lord I grew excited at God's healing mercy. I asked about the baby and the nurses kept telling me the baby's name. Baby Don, baby Don they kept saying they repeated as they moved in slow motion tending their patients.

I walked out from the clinic with a sense of pride at God's miraculous handiwork. Only to have our translator tell me that the nurses in their limited English were trying to tell me, "Baby gone, Baby dead."

The Wishing Children

The wells stood disappointed
They had no water to satiate the wishing children
The fires went back to sleep
They had no heat to warm the wishing children.
The ground moaned in grief
It had no seeds to feed the wishing children
Smiles changed their minds
Laughter was not to be wasted on whizzing children
Brains went into hibernation
Undernourished for the long winter's nap
The earth opened wide
It ate hungrily the children
Who no longer could wish.
"Empty"

CHAPTER TWENTY THREE
HERE'S TO HAITI

Promise Rain

Ker-plop!
Ker-plunk!
Plit-plit-plit-plit-plit-plit-plit-plit
It rained huge Haitian
Texas sized drops
Perpendicular to the ground
Surrounding us with the
Sound of bacon frying in
A humungous skillet
Encompassing us with a strong coffee smell of
Sizzling wet earth
Suddenly…
Simultaneously as if on cue
Children rushed out in the rain
Buckets appeared from everywhere
Littering the earth
To catch the fresh water
A promise from the grocery store of heaven.

Night Orchestra

Masterful God
Directs the night orchestra
Anointing sleep to soothe away
The worries and lack of the day
Children dream of food
Mothers dream of medicines and
Mothers dream of the dead fathers
Of their children
Living down the mountain
With other women.
God conducts the night
Covering the expected horrors of tomorrow
"one"
A young boy in a family of 9 counts
One…one…one…
The one mango he has
Over and over again
One…one…one…
'til he falls asleep

I See

I see a promised people
Overflowing with the milk and honey
Of dignity and grace
Their lives pared down to
The real human side of the human race

Tones

Symphonic earth shades
Blending in with
The harmonic Haitian Sisterscapes
Skin tones of
Ebony green
Hinted hues of midnight mauve
Monochromatic African rainbows
Deep blue browns
Black burgundies
A melodic blend of Mother Earth's people

Hot Haitian Nights

Sleep adjustments are difficult
In the hot Haitian nights,
Sighing and pillow punching
Tossing and turning
Finally I have sweated enough to
Create a cool spot in which to fall or stumble asleep…
With the sweetness of His son's name
God sprinkles comforting dreams
Of family and homeland
Abruptly
God's night shift sonata ends
His orchestral darkness chased away
By the sudden lone jazz cry of a brazen grandfather
Donkey who brays
Hee-haw, hee-haw, GO AWAY DARK!
He repeats his call to the north
Hee-haw, hee-haw, GO AWAY DARK!
To the east
Hee-haw, hee-haw GO AWAY DARK1
To the west
Hee-haw, hee-haw GO AWAY DARK!
Another donkey friend attaches, harmonizing
More brother donkeys and uncle donkeys
Hee-haw, hee-haw, hee-haw
Destroying the remainder of my night
A long legged lean dog

Angry, too, at his disturbed sleep
Knowing it is 4 in the morning, time to get up
Fusses at the dark he barks
DON'T BE LAZY DARK GO AWAY
DON'T BE LAZY DARK GO AWAY
A hungry barely there baby donkey nudges his mommy
Begging for breakfast
He whisper brays
Getuuuuuuuup-getuuuuuuuup-heehaaaaw-heehaaaaaw.
The night silence has vanished
Completely replaced by hawking birds
And finally
Rooster after rooster after rooster
Interrupted by the scurrying of full grown
Malnourished piglets
Racing each other to be the first for their morning mud bath
All of my Americaness begs not to get up
My head now buried under my hot pillow for an hour
5 o'clock in the morning
I stumble to my knees
And beg God's forgiveness for the new day dawning.

The Beauty of Haiti

The fog actually sat in my hand
Amazing morning puffs of
Angel dust hovering, gliding, sliding and bumbling
As heavenly overflow
Spilling on the earth fields
Released to wander and roam
For a brief moment on their own
Dominating this unevenly earthly home
Then poof!
Inhaled by the sun to return
Sliding through the pearly gates
As splendid pillow cushions
Upon which the angels may once again
Lay their heads.
"I have fallen mad-deep in love
with a people and with a place"

Chapter Twenty Three

"...You Bring Dem More Hope?"

When first I arrived
The children stood before me
Absent
Absent of goals
Absent of worthy endeavors.
Absent of child like presence
That is the reflection
I saw in the eyes of the children.
Absence
When first I arrived in Haiti.
Now
10 years later
When first I arrive
The children run and leap through the equatorial heat
Chasing my truck,
Yelling and shouting at me
Singing praise at me,
"YES, JESUS LOVE ME!" they bellow.
"Mix Yolanda", the ebony leathered driver
shines with a toothless smile,
"the children are happy to see you again, mam,
Every time you come you bring them more hope."
I have found that my Jesus-like presence
Gives them back their presence of childhood.

The Holiness of a Shower Curtain

The church was overflowing full
As the people "Ahmin-ed" their Amens
Facing the pulpit whose back drop
Was a plastic shower curtain
They sang and sang and sang
Lifting the invisible roof that stretched
Touching heaven's floor
Sitting skin overlapping skin
To get everybody in
The overflow people were the stained glass window panes
As they listened and listened and listened
Standing room only
To the preacher man who spoke a language
One they could understand
As the people "Ahmin-ed" their Amens
Facing the pulpit whose back drop was a shower curtain
I imagined
My church back home
Where the congregation choked in silence on their praise
And the windows were stained with glass
And the ceiling was acoustically correct
To accommodate the silence
As the preacher preached in front
Of an intricate museum inspired mural
Of Jesus with sad eyes
embracing an even sadder eyed baby lamb

CHAPTER TWENTY THREE

I stood and shouted AMEN
The Haitian people "Ahmin-ed" my Amen
And I didn't want the church service to end
As I faced the pulpit, whose backdrop was
A Holy shower curtain.

DO YOU KNOW WHOOPI GOLDBERG?

As I was teaching the young children
Wearing my hair in a multitude of long braids
A teenaged boy staring at me
Leaning his torso inside
Through the glassless window
Sabotaged my concentration
None of my students seemed bothered.
All of the windows were full of faces
Perched in the openings like night owls
Watching my every move
They had only seen white missionaries from America
I was their first
Their first African American female
"You know Whoopi Goldberg?"
The lad leaning in the window boldly shouted.
I wanted to say yes
Because it seemed like the boy
Really needed me to know her
But that would have been a lie
And missionaries don't lie
It seemed that his point of reference
For African American women
Was based on a cinema he once saw
Of Whoopi Goldberg

CHAPTER TWENTY FOUR

In Port-au-Prince
A city with electricity.
I walked over to the window.
I told the inquisitive lad
"No, I don't know Whoopi Goldberg,
But I love her movies."
And it was just as I thought.
He looked disappointed in me
In his eyes
I had no clout,
I remembered the adage "It's all in who you know"
He turned from the window
And stalked away
I turned from the window and
Continued to teach
I am confounded that one of
the perceived stereotypes in a remote mountain village in
Haiti of a black woman from America is
Whoopi Goldberg.
I must meet Whoopi and tell her
This is something worth her knowing.

I could not help but fall in love with the people, people like any other people, wanting what every culture of people wants. To love and be loved, to protect and be protected, to provide and to be provided for. Wanting--validation, dignity, grace and a sense of integrity. The same prescription that soothed all of my aches and pains and boosted my joys and victories.

CHAPTER TWENTY FIVE
THE APPLE

Finally another African American woman. An African American woman of color on the mission field. She's a nurse. We've been here 3 days and have barely said a word to each other, we've been so busy. She came as part of the medical team. She tends to the flesh. I tend to the soul. So our paths never crossed until

The Apple

She scurried in a brisk hurry from the clinic
With the deliberate step
Of a woman in trouble seeking
Another woman in her likeness
Who understood our history
We conspired desperately
No time for social amenities,
hello, how are you are whazzup
She cut to the chase
"I gave out my last apple."
"Apple? Where did you get an apple?"
I whispered in awe.

"They were my apples for on the plane. But I've discovered in seeing all of these patients, what ails my patients stems from drinking unclean water and a lifetime of malnutrition. I've been emptying my purse of my personal food that I brought from America. It's all gone. Help me!"

"I've given all of my personal food out too. I had cheese and nuts and twizzlers."

"Nuts?"

"A can of Cashews. But they're gone."

We stood close, breast to breast, brow to brow, our souls entangled, her heart begging mine.

"I have some cereal still for my children in Vacation Bible School."

"Get it now! I have a starving dying child in my office and my purse is empty."

Enough said. No questions asked, only the transference of urgency from her heart to mine. I sprinted, chased by my lack of faith. Will I have enough tomorrow for the children in Vacation Bible School? They too are starving.

The Voice spoke. "A child is dying now! I have empowered you to fix it now."

I ran faster. I stuffed my back pack full of baggies of cereal. I ran back to my soul sister and dropped the pack at her feet. She turned, as if lifted by the wind, her feet barely touching the ground, swift as Paul Revere, she ran her precious cargo back to her make shift ward.

I walked slowly, following her path, toward the clinic. I looked more closely at the people, my people. I gazed into the deep set eyes of starvation. I was hypnotized by the African Haitian DNA that spoke volumes to my African American DNA. My people are dying...now. Pivoting, angrily, I stalked back to my room and grabbed another back pack and stood before the bin, knowing it was only half full of cereal, barely enough to feed the 600 mouths for the last 2 days of VBS.

I removed the lid and...GLORY...IT WAS FULL. Every time I reached in the bin to fill my back pack, the cereal shifted and the bin remained full. This was the first time my mustard seed missionary

THE APPLE

faith relied on God's bounty and he supplied fully, beyond my wild-est imaginings. I felt the smile of The Voice embracing me. This didn't just happen once…oh the miracles I could tell.

"The air smelled sweet with the smell of the hungry children crunch-crunch-crunching."

CHAPTER TWENTY SIX
SIX

6:40 a.m.

I am very, very excited and early. I step in the classroom. I get shivers from my toes to the very roots of my hair. The small classroom is already amazingly full of children. However, I was soon to discover that, by Haitian standards, the classroom was empty. Upon seeing me, the children freeze like in a black and white school picture or a sepia toned movie still. The children with their charcoal brown pipe cleaner arms and balloon like bellies, are eerily quiet, their protruding eyes fixed on me. I knew they were waiting for me to say something, but the translator hadn't arrived and I don't speak an inkling of Creole. I nodded. They nodded. I nodded again. Again they solemnly nodded back at me...me...their "Teechuh" from America.

6:45 a.m.

A huge crowd of children exploded into the room, hustling, with volcano like explosiveness as if they were late. Seeing me, they slapped, nudged and poked one another into silence, then they tiptoed their energy into their learning spaces. 6:45. Class was still not scheduled to start for an hour and 15 minutes. The children sat, motionless, poised and ready. There is no way in America that this many children would ever be this quiet or well behaved. I watched them carefully watching me. I smile. They smile even bigger. I wink. They wink and those who had never winked before cascaded into giggling as they tried to make their eyes cooperate. They began testing their new skill on one another and the room became full of the carnival sounds of universal laughter. They began to talk amongst themselves. Children sounds, like in America that I'm familiar with. Joy abruptly shut herself down. All eyes guiltily turned toward the entry into the classroom. In glides François, the School Administrator, my translator and my dear, dear friend. He arrives roughly ushering in 2 little ones. "We mustn't be late," he announces for the whole classes benefit. He majestically surveys the children. His eye landscapes them into perfect obedience.

"Good morning." He says to me officially. He points to the children he escorted into the room. "Dey are budder and sistuh. He cannot speak." I eye the two as they squeeze into a spot where there is no spot. The brother is small, seeming to be about 6, and the sister looked to be 3 or 4. With all of the poverty in the mountains, I knew the boy would easily be 12 and the girl 8. It is like that in Haiti.

7:45 a.m.

I begin giving each child a snack bag full of cereal. There are now 54 students in attendance in a room where if it had been America, would have been meant to accommodate 25...thirty at the max.

"Crunch, crunch, crunch!" The only sound in the room. If only...

One of these big companies could drop boxes of cereal onto the mountains

If only...

I could get a plane and a pilot

When supplies are mailed or shipped they very rarely make it this far up the mountain

They end up stolen in Port-au-Prince, that is if they don't disappear first in Miami. The cruel reality is that the children get only the supplies that I am able to physically carry on my back. Unfortunate-

Six

ly this is not only dictated by the airline weight restrictions but also dictated by the status of my 55 plus year old body.

If only…

The air smelled sweet with the smell of the hungry children crunch-crunch-crunching.

8:00 a.m.

Time to teach.

"English. Only English. You will only speak in English today with Miss Yolantha," sternly announces François.

The non-speaking brother watches me with such intensity that I deduce that he can at least hear me. His eyes follow intently every move I make. He shifts his hands around his little sister's waist who, for lack of space, sits on his lap. His hands catch my attention. To my astonishment on the side of each of his pinky fingers protrudes another tiny finger about the size of my baby toe. The child has six fingers on each hand. I introduce myself.

"I am Mrs. Pace. I live in Kentucky. I have 2 dau--"

"Wait for me, wait for me," interrupts François. He translates into Creole for the children,

"2 daughters named Erin and Diamond. I love them and miss them very, very much."

François translates. I begin the lesson. The children are instructed to repeat after me. They delight and chuckle at the pictures in my book. Even the speechless boy's little sister participated with delight.

"On page one we have one apple. A is for apple." I announce holding up 1 finger.

"Repeat!" commands François.

"Un payege won weh ha wun appoo. A is fuh appoo" they grin.

"Apple." I say.

"Appoo" they say.

"Ah-puuuuullllllll" says François.

"Ahhhhhhh-puuuuullllllllllll" imitate the children.

I show them the picture. Their eyes glisten. I cannot tell if it is with hunger or with delight.

"On page 2 we have 2 birds. B is for birds" I now hold up 2 fingers.

"Repeat!" commands François.

"Un payege two weh ha two budz. B is fuh budz". The children hold up 2 fingers.

"Birds", I correct.

"Budz" they say.

"burr-burr-burrr" I correct

"buh-buh-buh" they say.

This is going to take a while. "On page three we have 3 cars. C is for cars"

"On payege three we ha-"

"Have" I interrupt

"ha"

"Have!"

"HA"

"vuh, vuh, vuh. Hav-vuh" I try harder.

"hah----vuh"

"HAVE!" I frown.

"Hah-VUH-VUH-VUH!" they frown.

"HAVE!" I frown deeper.

"Hah-vuh" they scowl, more determined, mimicking and trying to please me.

I surrender and move on. They repeat after me all morning trying to duplicate my English. Only the translator speaks in Creole. We made it to page 5 with 5 elephants and the letter E, the 5th letter of the alphabet. I showed them the picture on the next page and I told them all that tomorrow we will start on page 6 with the 6th letter of the alphabet.

Six

7:45 a.m.
The next morning.

I had decided not to arrive as early as yesterday. I approach the class room door. It swings open and a huge wave of children splash me with, "WELKUM TEECHUCH!!!" I enter into a cloud of toilet paper, the gorgeous brown hues of their bodies sparkling in the snow white contrast.

In America the room would have been decorated with crepe paper and streamers, but here I was greeted with drape after drape after drape of toilet tissue. My heart leaped with joy at the pristine sight. My memory blazed back to the very first and only other time I'd been tee-peed. It was for Halloween. I was 11 years old. We had just moved to Champaign, Illinois that summer and were living in an all white neighborhood. In 1966 my family and I were the first "Negroes" to integrate our block. There was a family across the street and two houses down who hated us, absolutely detested us. All of the other kids learned to love us because draped over our entire front yard was a gigantic weeping willow tree. A huge billowing tree better known to our new friends as--the fort, the playhouse, the palace, Piggly Wiggly's, the dungeon or what ever imaginary world suited us that day.

That first Halloween in Champaign, some time in the middle of the night our neighbors--the ones who hated us, who lived across the street and two houses down had toilet papered our tree. Not just a toss here or there, but a painstaking, meticulous, complete covering of our tree. It was a glorious work of art. They had transformed our huge weeping willow tree into a gigantic Alaskan igloo. I stood at our front door awestruck. What a magnificent welcoming gesture of status for all of the neighborhood to see. It was absolutely beautiful. I couldn't wait to get home from school and let our imaginations run wild in perhaps an imaginary game of "the north pole".

Imagine how dumbfounded I was to hear the whispers later on at school. Finally my brother slapped the secret grin off of my face when he explained to me that the message intended by the alleged "disgracing" of our tree, was "Niggers go home." From 1966 to this very day. I've lived in denial. Because I refuse to believe that anything so heavenly beautiful could ever be intended for something so ugly.

My memories were interrupted by the angelic avalanche of young voices, jam packed into a room meant to hold only 25, thirty at the most, singing.

"We're so hahpy, so very hahpy, so very hahpy to see you to daaaaay"

Ah the power of toilet paper to bring me supreme joy. The children from yesterday had multiplied. They were now standing sideways in order to fit. François and I counted 152 bodies. What would the fire marshals say in America? But this is Haiti.

At a signal from François they all sit with faces torpedoed toward me with huge expectant smiles, anxious for another day of learning. Quickly I pass out baggies of cereal. There were so many children, I had to return to my room to get more. As they were crunching I asked in English, "what page are we on today?" the smiles evaporate. The whole class stares at me with the same eyes of children in America when they haven't remembered their lesson from the day before.

"Who remembers?" I ask. "Nobody? Nobody remembers???" Angrily, I placed my hands on my African American hips. François, his brows furrowed in disappointment places his hands on his African Haitian hips and translates my frustration to the children in Creole.

"Aaaaaaach!" I growl, and turn my back.

"Aaaaaaach!" imitates François and turns his back.

Six

"Teechu we will start on payeege six," says a raspy quiet voice. I look over my shoulder, it is the little boy holding his sister tightly in his lap.

"Very good." I encouraged, pretending that the little boy always spoke. "Let's go back to page one. What is on page one?"

"One apoo and o beige two, two birds, " announces the young lad. "Paygee three, three cats, page foh, foh dogs, page five, five eleephuhtz,."

"And on page 6?" I asked.

The little boy smiled sharing every tooth that he owned. He held up one of his hands, then proclaimed with confidence, "and on payeege six we have six finguhs."

I could smell the sweet smell of hope in the room. I knew then that I was in this to the point of no return.

"Like Mathew, Mark, Luke, and John."

CHAPTER TWENTY SEVEN
THE STORY OF APPLESAUCE

One Sunday afternoon I was walking with some teenage boys. We were returning from the Sabbath services at Jehovah Jireh. A church service done entirely in English so that the teenage youth can practice their language skills. As we walked, I decided to help them practice their English. Of course, I began with my old American standby.

"What do you guys want to be when you grow up." They grinned and grinned and grinned. The joy of being able to practice their English with an American was their ultimate highlight of the day.

"I want to work on computahs."

"I want to be a tee chair"

Then one young guy said, "I want to be applesauce."

"Applesauce?…Applesauce?" I asked.

Johnson one of my best student translators spoke louder on behalf of his best friend as if I were deaf, just like we do to the Mexicans and foreigners in America.

"APPLE SAUCE--AH-POL--SAUCE."

"Applesauce???"…I still didn't understand.

Leaning in my face, Johnson spoke even louder.

"AHHHHHHH-POOOOOOOOOOOOOO-SAUCE--LIKE JOH AND MATTEW IN DE BIBOH." He spoke loudly to make sure I understood.

"John and Matthew? Matthew and John…Boohoo you want to be an apostle! You want to grow up to be an apostle?" My guts wanted to explode with laughter, my eyeballs began to involuntarily water with merriment. I twisted my tongue every way I could. I folded my lips inside my mouth, then pushed them out into a kissie-poo-pucker. "Apostle, not apple sauce. Apple sauce is like a food we make from the fruit to feed babies. We mash an aaaaaaaaaaaah," I lost it. I started laughing and couldn't get control.

In all of my 50 something years of living, no one has ever told me that they wanted to grow to be an apostle. I nicknamed my friend from then on Applesauce. Who is Applesauce? My dear, dear friend Andronic. And from that day on, he has tried desperately to improve his English. And from that day on, I have tried desperately to improve my hearing.

CHAPTER TWENTY EIGHT
EVERYBODY NEEDS A FRIEND LIKE JOHNSON

Johnson is definitely hands down my best student interpreter. Johnson had been translating for the missionaries for at least 2 years. He was one of François' best pupils. Applesauce, aka Andronic, is Johnson's best friend. But Andronic's English is not developed enough for the missionaries to choose him as a translator.

"Mix Yolantha, applesauce is very disappointed." Johnson began to plead his friends case. "He has no father Mix Youlahnda, many brothers and sister, no source of income." This was the typical scenario.

"Andronic, my friend, your applesauce, is needing money to help pay for his brothers to go to school. Applesauce does anything he can for his family." Johnson said, "applesauce works hard to get a little food for his family and then doesn't have food for himself so I give him some of mine."

I remember the first year I came. Johnson was an excruciatingly, skinny skeleton of a young lad. Just like all of my other students. Johnson stood out from all of the other starving children because he always turned down snacks. "No thank you miss," he would say avoiding making eye contact. After three days of this I begged.

"Please eat."

"I cannot eat, when my family , my brother, at home will not have food. It is not right for me to be able to eat if my brother cannot eat." He spoke like a true revolutionist. That was over 7 years ago. Johnson was just 11 years old then. Now he is 19.

"Go get your brother so he too can eat." I told my little eleven year old warrior.

The next day Johnson proudly introduced me to John Smith. His twin.

Now again, 11 years later I noticed Johnson did not partake of snacks. I wondered if it was because his best friend Andronic wasn't going to have snack, since he was not one of my translators. My spirit said that Johnson, once again in Gandhi fashion was pleading the case for his friend just as Jesus pleads the case for me. However no matter what Johnson did, Applesauce's English was not good enough to convince the missionaries to use him as a translator. However that year we had so many children in Vacation Bible School that I was able to get him hired as one of my helpers. He became one of my disciplinarians. Now Johnson and his friends Applesauce aka Andronic were able to join me for snack each day.

CHAPTER TWENTY NINE
NOT YET

François is the superintendent of schools for 23 schools and over 5,000 children in the Pignon, Ranquitte area. He is the proctor for academic test groups. He is the father of 4. He is the epitome of dignity , integrity and love for his people. He is not just my translator , he is my friend. He is truly my right hand as well as my ears, my tongue and my heart.

He prepares the children every morning for my arrival. He is like the warm up comedienne for David Letterman or the warm up band before the main attraction. Every morning when I arrive to teach, the children are bright, alert and ready. We laugh, cry, plan and provide together for the children of Haiti.

After Breakfast

My belly is full American style after breakfast
I hop, skip, run, perform just like in America,
I teach full of energy for the children of Haiti.
After lunch
I'm abundantly, blindly full of
Home made bread, eggplant casserole,
Beans, heaping mounds of rice,
Fresh garden tomatoes, plantains,
Chunks of Velveeta cheese
And slice, after slice, after slice
Of fresh off the tree
Sweet, succulent, elbow dripping

CHAPTER TWENTY NINE

Finger licking
Mangos.
Mangos like I've never tasted in America.
Rejuvenated, I'm ready once again
To hop, skip, run, perform and teach just like in America
Full of energy for the children of Haiti
Yet there is such lethargy among my translators and helpers
At the end of the day
I scolded them for their lack of pep and zip and energy
On the second day,
I was full of a bountiful cornucopia of food
and zest after my noon feast
It was 2:00
I was satiated and armed to teach
François, my dear friend and translator
Was holding his head up with his hand
Blurry eyed, repeating after me in a tired
Monotone Creole fashion
My Haitian students too imitated him
In a lazy daisy tired monotone Creole fashion
At my wits end, frustrated,
With a slip of the tongue
Concerning François having had lunch,
I mistakenly asked,
"Have you not had breakfast, François?"
"No missus, Yolantha, not yet."
I froze recognizing my error
Yet amazed at his response.
I stopped breathing.
"Did you have breakfast yesterday?"
"No Missus Yolantha, not yet."
Still holding my breath

NOT YET

"have you had breakfast this week?"
"No missus, not yet."
I was stripped of my Christianity right then and there.
My head knows and my brain knows that
I am in one of the poorest countries in the world.
I see daily the distended bellies and
Reddish blondish malnutrition hair.
I see the water that we as Americans aren't able to drink
Laundered in, urinated in by the donkeys,
Cooked with by the women.
I've witnessed dying dehydrated
Tearless babies
But in my religiosity
In my goody goodness
In my American callousness,
In my Jim crowed-slavery mentality
In my Rodney King
Sister of lynched brothers
In my institutionalized callousness--
Until now
It was all National Geographic to me.
But the "not yet" stripped me of my ungodly ways
It was the "hope" that stands tall in the
"NOT YET"
Now the power of hope was in my hands
How does one make a difference in a country full of
"not yets?"
Every day from that moment on
I stuffed food in my pockets for my friend,
my brother François.

Memo to Self

Sunday evening
I slid the peanuts off of my plate into my pocket
Monday morning
I gave the nuts to François.
Monday evening
In my pocket I stuffed a chunk of bread
and pulled off a handful of Velveeta cheese
Tuesday morning
I provided breakfast of Velveeta Cheese and bread
For my translator and friend, François
"You have nuts for me Missus Yolantha?"
"No not today"
Memo to self,
"hmmm, so now we're putting in orders for breakfast?"
Memo to missionary self,
"Remember the nuts tomorrow."
Tuesday evening
I use my finger to scoop out peanut butter
on a chunk of homemade bread
Wednesday morning
François my translator and friend
Slowly accepts my offering of peanut butter
and homemade bread
"no nuts today Missus Yolantha?"
sadly asks François, my translator and friend.
"No not today." I heard my American upbringing

NOT YET

unchaining itself in the dungeon of my heart.
"Beggars can't be choosy"
rattled around in the depths of my lungs,
but for the Grace of God did not slip past my lips.
Wednesday evening
I made it from the table with Velveeta cheese,
Fried bananas, 2 chunks of homemade bread,
And a hand full of nuts
Thursday morning
"Ah nuts," exclaimed François with a huge grin,
"thank you so much Missus Yolantha."
He scurries away like a squirrel
with his proud prize of Planters peanuts
On my way to join François
I pass
Long lines of people
Standing waiting outside of the clinic
They are 2 hours early
Before the doors even open
It reminds me of when I once stood
In the food stamp line in America
Memo to self
Next year I must try
To provide food for the
Long lines of people
Waiting for the clinic to open.
My soul cringes
"Next year!"
That's 365 days of "Not yets"
365 days of hoping.
Arriving a few minutes early to teach
I make my grand entrance,

CHAPTER TWENTY NINE

Unexpected, I stepped into the classroom
There was François preparing the children,
François was walking around the jam packed,
Over crowded classroom
That broke every municipal school building rule
and fire code in America
Handing out to every child
ONE peanut.
Every child's hand quietly outstretched waiting with hope
Their only breakfast in months.
Memo to American self"
"Is there a rung on the ladder lower than humbled?"

What kind of hope was I providing in the name of my Father who owns the cattle on a thousand hills and the meadows with acres of peanuts?

Jeeeeeeeeeeeeeeeeeeeeeeeeeeezuuuuuuuuuuuuuuuuuus!!!

CHAPTER THIRTY
WATCHING FROM AMERICA

My heart doesn't fit in my body, it's crowding my lungs, there is no room for breath. There are no curse words even to express my feelings as I recall about "NOT YET".

I barely had a handle on hope before the earthquake. This earthquake has completely upset my apple cart.

"Whose apple cart is it anyway?"

It's God again. I hear a low snarl in the pit of my stomach and a hissing sound escapes as I exhale. I grope riffling desperately through my blue books. Avoiding the answer.

"Feed my sheep."

"A peanut???? A peanut??? What am I doing?

The Rainy Season Comes Early
(March 2010, in America)

Scoop and pour
Scoop and pour
Sweep-sweep-sweep
Scoop and pour
Scoop and pour
Sweep-sweep-sweep
I watched
as the two women
tried to keep the rain water
from entering their tent

made of a queen sized
fitted sheet.
Scoop.
Sweep-sweep-sweep.
In slow motion
I pick up the remote
and turn off CNN.
It's all wrong.

I Need to Cry

I can't do this God? I need you. I watched CNN The woman was scooping Tupperware after Tupperware scoops of rain from in front of her brand new drooping home made of...sheets. I need you, she needs you, we need you God more than ever. I thought we had done something, something, grandiose in the past 9 years on the mission field. I look at my earthquaked Haiti. I need to cry. But tears wouldn't solve anything. I knew a different Haiti. Different. We in America have no point of reference for the things I have seen in Haiti. I've seen poor in America. In America the poorest of the poor can only afford one vowel and one consonant. "Po" as we say down south. I've seen an old curmudgeon of a black man burrowed in the corner of his refrigerator box on the streets of California. I've seen a woman retrieving a half eaten sandwich in the trash outside of the Greyhound bus station in St. Louis. I've seen an over sized coated man wearing all of his clothing pushing a grocery cart full of greasy bags and 3 folding chairs in Harlem. I've been in homes in Houston in the 3rd Ward where rats and roaches had first choice. I've visited my own relatives whose homes have never ever seen a coat of paint. But I had never seen poverty up close and personal like the poverty I hugged, kissed and ministered to in Haiti. I used to see smidgeons of it on those "savethechildrenfeedthechildren" 4 a.m. TV shows. But there are no coffee breaks, windows to Windex, Maytag, Verizon versus AT&T commercial breaks in Haiti. The pre-quake Haiti. Pigeon holed as the poorest nation in the western hemisphere. Now, since the earthquakes, we can brag and boast and toast. "HERE'S TO HAITI...the poorest nation in the world."

I climb onto my computer chair. I retrieve my blue books. I keep my bluebooks hidden on a top shelf in two State Fair Pancakes 'n Sausage boxes. I can almost taste my blood as it rushes from my heart to my head and back down again. Haiti needs me to make an INTENTIONAL difference. A RIGOROUS difference. I am needed more now than ever (me...that's a scary thought). I go into the bathroom, lean real close, my nose touching my nose in the mirror. Me.

Millions, over half a billion dollars worth of supplies and foods and materials have been sent. François Filogene, my translator and friend. The superintendent of schools, my best friend in the whole of Haiti and maybe even in all of America, my friend hasn't seen a penny. Some of those were his pictures, our pictures, from God's work on the George Clooney international telethon. Yet none of my "models of poverty" have seen one tent, one bottle of water, one comb, one kernel of rice; one penny.

François Are You There?

My brain scorches back to the evening of January 12th when I first found out.

I tommy gunned my computer:

6:39

Dearest François, heard about the earth quake

Are you okay?

7:00

François,

Looking to hear from you.

Are you okay?

7:52

François?

Are you okay?

9:03

ARE you okay?

9:50

Are YOU okay?

10:11

Are you OKAY?

Midnight

OKAY????? I typed in like a stalking and frustrated lover.

January 13, 2:00 a.m.

I type, "François?" I sit in front of my computer and bump my head on the back of my chair, like I used to do as a little pigtailed child on my pillow after getting a whipping for something I didn't do. Just like then, I pounded till I, exhausted from crying, fell asleep.

January 13, 6:53 p.m.

There it was. A note from François.

"I cannot be OK when most of my fellow citizens are in desperate straits. They are in dire needs for shelter, food medications, clothing, clean water to drink. I wonder if Haiti is the most unfortunate country in the world. It is the country where most people are in extreme poverty if I don't want to say--in absolute poverty. WE are devastated emotionally. We are in complete fear. WE are scared to death because we don't know what will happen to destroy the rest of the population. Our situation becomes more critical. Now we are in an incomparable situation. We cry for help. We don't know what to do. Please help us. Please help us. Please help us. WE are really in needs."

And my François, translator and friend signs off, "God keep on blessing AMERICA."

March 21, 2010

It's been over a month now, millions upon millions of dollars have been donated and Superintendent of Schools, François Filogene, my friend, has not seen one Band-Aid, one aspirin, one sock, one doll. I hunt down and put on my Wal-mart combat boots, I turn off the TV, closet myself in front of my computer…armed with my pancake boxes…bluebooks as ammunition…with John Wayne determination and the true grit of Maya Angelou I stick out my chin and begin again. NOBODY KNOWS THE HAITI I'VE SEEN.

"Where am I?
In a land where ketchup is 7 American Dollars"

NOBODY KNOWS THE HAITI I'VE SEEN

I Saw Haiti

I saw a baby staring
with ancient eyes
As a mother washed its face
In the creek
where other women
Pounded their cloth pieces clean
Down from a boy
who washed his teeth
Three feet away
from his ragged donkey
Who stood in the creek
relieving himself
I saw Haiti.

Dead Girls

Young dead girls
Play listlessly in the leaves
No tomorrow challenges
No lost love songs
Just another aimless dead day
Followed by another and another
A multitude of hopeless
Dead undreamed of days
Now old dead girls
Sweep listlessly in the leaves.

Universal Languages

Finding a way to relate
Finding a common thread
My tools?
A smile
Laughter
Music
A hug
Where there is no language
The universal spirit must speak
The subtleness of my body language reveals
The loudness of my silent attitudes
How versed am I in the unspoken dialects
How sincere is my smile
How loving is my laughter
How musical is my heart
How embracing is my hug?

Hopelessness

We arrive
The people gather
Along the briar fences posed as
Painted statues of poverty
The children move in slow motion
In the equatorial heat
Their ample lips hang loosely
Their eyes gaze like the elderly
I visit in the nursing homes of America
Who have resigned to a life
They have no control over
The children's emaciated hopelessness
Reflects like old folkness
What an amazing American mirror I see.

The Toy

The little boy
Full of joy
Waved his arm back and forth
Up and down
And around and around
His concentration intrigued me
So I had to move close to see
He played with a string
His only play thing
He snapped and wrapped
Dragged and tickled
Wiggly-wagged and wiggled
His only toy thing…
His string

The following Christmas, back in America, as I shopped for my daughters I thought of the little boy and his string. I thought of all of the myriad of unplayed with toys and gadgets and machines that I had purchased for my family.

I wondered if Santa
would bring a new string
for my little boy without a toy.
I hung my head and wept
as I looked at the multitude of toys
my Christmas tree kept.

Forever Encore

The Haitian man
Played multi-colored notes
Beckoning colored people
With instrument totes
Conducting a tempo
Of hues dancing
The prismatic rainbow
Sounds for romancing
Yellow notes played
Sun-kissed fandangos
Brown notes flamingoed
A big band tango
White notes strummed
Delicious dulcimer rounds
Black notes drummed
Lightening lion sounds
Green notes recycled
Earth saving stanzas anew
Red Cloud played totem poles
A denim sky blue
Royal purple sang
A majestic presidential tune
The peacock colored orchestra
Played way past high noon
Making raw music
Plucking in the full moon

Nobody Knows The Haiti I've Seen

The multi-colored man
Played multi-colored notes
As the children plaited his hair
In intricate shapes of baroque
And the angel's arpeggios relayed
"Tomorrow, today must be replayed"
They wrote, and sang with golden throats
"When the multi-colored Haitian man
Will once again play his multi-colored notes."

"Because you look like the people..."

CHAPTER THIRTY TWO
BEGGING

"**I** don't mean any harm, but because you look like the people, don't be surprised if they are all over you begging you for money. You especially are going to have to be careful." This was the advice from one of the white male missionaries as he sought to prepare me for my journey to Haiti.

As well meaning as this White American friend was, he could not have been farther from the truth. The very first time someone begged something from me, it was a little boy about the age of 10. He sidled up real close. He looked up longingly with the deepest of huge brown eyes.

"Mam...Mam...do you have a mat book?"

"A what?" I asked.

"A mat book. I cannot continue on in skule unless I have a good fondashun. I must get better in mat. Can you get me a mat book?"

I was floored. A math book? A child was begging me for a math book?

When I returned to America I combed the dollar stores for math work books to take back to Haiti. The following year upon my return, I presented the workbooks to the Haitian children as I traveled along the way, you would have thought I had given them gold.

The second time someone begged from me, it was once again a child. He asked for my suitcase.

"Mam, when it rains. We have a dirt flo. The rain gets into my home and all of my clothes (the one other outfit that he was not wearing) get wet. But if I had yo suitcase, there would be a way to keep all of my family's clothes dry."

And the third and only thing in the 10 years that I've served in Haiti that anyone ever begged me for--was a woman who begged me for my bra. She too was just wanting to have a "good foundation".

CHAPTER THIRTY THREE
HOME VISITS

In America

In America I trained to be on the home visitation outreach ministry for our church. I don't know what possessed me to join this ministry, because it was definitely something outside of my comfort zone. The focus of the ministry was to make people who had visited our church feel welcome by giving them a personal home visit with the hope that they would feel led to join our church. We were trained in how to sell our church and we were trained to be able to offer the plan of salvation to the lost souls that we might encounter. We learned scripture and we learned how to pray with people. One of the prayers that we were encouraged to pray was to ask the Holy Spirit to go before us and prepare the way for our visit. I remember thinking, "Dear God, please don't let anybody slam the door in my face and please God don't let them cuss me out." Because I knew at that point in my life, if those things happened, I wasn't sure that my immaturity as a Christian would be able to over ride my maturity as a sinner with an inner city mentality.

In reality, on most American home visits we mainly visited through porch screens or slipped people information about our church through a small crack in their door. On one very rare occasion, however; we were actually invited in.

I sat stiffly face to face on the edge of a man's over stuffed sofa. After about 10 minutes of uncomfortable makeshift conversation we fumbled awkwardly through the plan of salvation. With sweat beading up on my forehead we offered him an invitation to accept Jesus as his personal Lord and Savior. The man hem-hawed around and confessed he had a drinking problem and that he wasn't married to the woman secretly hiding out in the bedroom until we left. He confessed that he honestly wasn't ready to make a commitment to God until he fixed those things.

A gate seemed to spring open under my armpits causing my deodorant to vacate the premises. I thought, "Game over. Let's go. God, hurry and get me out of this man's house before my body odor takes over his living room." He was definitely more convicted in his sins than I was in his Salvation. I was startled at myself at how quickly I gave up. Later on as I lay in bed, I realized that Satan knew his job. I didn't know mine. I decided then and there. "Sorry God, home visits are not my calling. Good night."

In Haiti

The ministry of living the life of the GOOD NEWS gets put to the test on our home visits. Our visit sites are usually chosen by the Mayor of the area, or a local Pastor. On other occasions we just take off walking and where the Holy Spirit leads…we visit.

A successful home visit depends on how dead to ourselves we are and how alive we are to our relationship with the LIVING Lord. A productive visit depends on whether or not we have embraced the gift of empowerment that Jesus left for each of us prior to His ascension back to join His father on His Heavenly Throne. Time after time a home visit in Haiti hinges on the question, "Do I personally truly believe in the power and miracles of Jesus"

A victorious visit comes from listening to the pleas of the people and then evoking the Holy Spirit to use you to do something that will meet their needs. Even if it is going to take a miracle.

HOME VISITS

The Routine

If praying makes you uncomfortable, then you will not enjoy home visits or really understand what happens at home visits. On the surface a home visit consists of getting statistics about the family we are visiting, assessing their physical needs, praying for these needs and then giving them some beans and rice or food or toothpaste and soap or what ever we have been able to cram into our American backpacks. We ask to pray with the family, then we move on to another house and repeat the same process.

We travel with a translator. We will drive to a general location split into groups of 4 to 7 and then travel on foot. We begin by getting permission to come onto the property of the family that we are visiting. When permission is granted I say:

"Thank you for allowing us to come to your home. We come in the name of Jesus bringing you His love, His peace and His joy. How are you? How many people are in your family? Is everybody healthy?"

Usually we get a long list of ailments and pains.

"Do you use the clinic?

This is one of the areas where communication becomes a challenge. In 7 years I've not been able to find out how our clinic works. Initially I was told the clinic was free. Recently I was told by the missionary leaders that the people are expected to pay what they can, but no one is turned away. At least that is what I am told to my face. American to American. What actually happens I don't know. But I do know we make home visits to many, many people who are in desperate need of medical attention but will not go to our clinic for assistance. Their standard answer as to why?-- "we have no money to go."

I see devastating things on home visits. I encountered a man with a huge rotting hole on his leg the size of my hand, a blind woman with an eye infection and gnats and liquid oozing out of her eyes, a child with a huge burn on the back of her leg and her behind who had fallen into the fire while playing. All on top of the usual yellow fever and extreme malnutrition and vitamin deficiencies. One home had human skeletal remains in their back yard.

Free

I was so moved with compassion on these home visits that I began to write notes for family members to be seen at the clinic. I fight for the people I see and insist that anyone bearing a medical note from me, must be seen at our "free" clinic. At first this seemed to cause challenges with the clinic and some of the missionary leaders, but a day later some of the other missionaries began to write medical notes. That summer every person with a note, was honored with assistance at our "free" clinic.

The Jesus Spiel

It was just a routine, normal typical home visit. I was spouting off the questions and noting the typical answers as I shifted from foot to foot in the horrendous sun.

"May we have permission to visit your home today? We come in the name of Jesus bringing you His love, His Peace and His Joy. How are you? How many people are in your family? Is everybody healthy? Are the children in school? How old are they?" Yada, yada, yada. Something inside of me pricked my boredom. Breaking my routine, I turned to one of the children and asked her what was her favorite subject in school?

"Mat." she whispered meekly, using her best English.

"Math?" I smiled emphasizing the T-H. "My daughter, Diamond loves math." I say encouragingly once again emphasizing the T-H.

I turned back to the mother and father. It is very rarely that we get to visit with both a mother and father, and said, "May we give you some things we have brought with us?"

As quietly as her daughter she said, "Wee"

After handing out toothpaste, miniature hotel soaps and shampoos, large baggies of rice and beans, and some mix-matched children's clothing, I asked, "May we pray for you and your family? Do you have any special prayer requests?"

The woman's immediate response was: "I WANT TO KNOW JESUS."

My breath left me and I almost passed out in the Haitian heat. The woman must have thought I didn't hear her, she repeated:

"I Want to Know Jesus"

Holy Spirit Go Before Us

As we approached her home she raised her
Hands to the sky and shouted in Creole
She walked around in a circle
Over and over again
Hands lifted to the sky
Tears streaming down her face
Laughing, crying and shouting.
She reminded me of the old time women of my youth
In the Black churches in America
Speaking in tongues I couldn't understand
Shouting glory and Praises to God
"What is she saying?" I asked the translator.
The translator said

"She is saying, 'Praise God!
Thank you God!
For sending the missionaries to my home!"
And even before we could give her the meager rice and beans
She was on her hands and knees
begging to accept Jesus Christ as
Her Lord and Savior.

There Are No Words

As the economy worsens in America, it worsens to an even greater extent in Haiti. Their government is not accountable to a binding constitution that provides social reforms. Haiti is not bound by civil rights amendments, free education and the pursuit of happiness clauses.

Every time I return to America I am at a loss of what to say, what to ask. There are no words in most American's vocabulary to describe what I see...pieces of a man's leg, hard and shiny as a leather jacket I once owned, surrounding a gaping hole full of greenish purplish rotting skin...a blind woman's eyes encrusted with what reminded me of potato chip crumbs, matted and feasted on by flies... children so emaciated standing before me in 3-D, as if they have stepped out from the TV at 4:00 in the morning from one of those FEED THE CHILDREN infomercials. Swollen bellies on multitudes of children as if they were 9 months pregnant. Children who are 9 months long over due with hunger.

CHAPTER THIRTY FOUR
I DON'T BELIEVE IN VOODOO

*We are told that 96% of the people practice voodoo.
We are also told that some of the religious leaders that
say that they are Catholic priests and Christian pastors are
also practicing voodoo priests*

Uncle McCoy

The man looked just exactly like my fathers deceased brother, my Uncle McCoy…frightfully so…the spitting image…his fraternal twin bother. It is said that Haiti is one of the last islands touched by the slave ships as a dumping ground for damaged goods; a dumping ground for defective cargo. It was the dumping ground for the slaves that were too sick to bring good money in America. They were dumped and left to die; another gut wrenching separation of families. My own immediate ancestry that survived the Middle Passage horrors ended up in Texas. We were initially cotton picking slaves.

However, as God would have it, many of the discarded Africans did not die. I'd noticed some of the people in Haiti looked just like me. Not the preverbal "all black folks look alike" syndrome. But I stare at people that look just like an intimate part of my DNA.

We called Uncle McCoy, Tippy, because of the way he walked. Uncle Tippy had contracted an unknown and untreatable disease while he served in the Korean War. When he returned from Korea he walked as if he had cerebral palsy…tipping on his left foot, then lifting his left shoulder in the air followed by the hoisting of his chest in order to pull his right leg along. And there, on this home visit, squatting before me was my dead Uncle Tippy's identical look alike, thousands of miles from Texas, in a remote Haitian mountain village.

The translator said, "This man has been stuck in this position for a long, long time. He cannot stand and walk"

The nurse in our visiting group asked the translator to ask the family what happened to him. A long explanation came forth from the family, but the translator responded with one word.

"Voodoo."

The other missionaries standing beside me gasped. I kicked myself in the heart and reminded myself for the umpteenth time, I must learn Creole. I squinted my eyes at the translator. I burrowed into him the way my mother used to do to me when she knew I wasn't telling her the whole truth.

"Tell me every thing that was said."

I felt our translator, a Christian, was often at war with the realities of his village and his empowerment to share only what he felt the missionaries needed to know. What our translator shared gave me one of my first true glimpses of voodoo.

"This man's brother was a voodoo priest. A very important man in the voodoo community. When his brother died the next day this man was cursed with the inability to stand."

The nurse with us went over to the man and took him firmly by the hands and tried to pull him to a standing position. He got partially unfurled and then snapped back into a squatting position like a rubber band. Our nurse's diagnosis was that he probably had been in the position so long that his muscles had atrophied, keeping him locked into a squatting position. I gave the man a granola bar, still entranced with how he looked so much like my Uncle Tippy. He ate the granola bar in slow motion.

The translator continued, "When a powerful person in voodoo dies, the people believe that the voodoo spirit looks for somewhere else to go. In this situation it went from the deceased brother to this brother."

As I later entered this event into my journal it, like now, sounded too ludicrous to even write down. But it boils down to the power of the mind to make the heart believe almost anything. Or is it the power of the heart to make the mind believe almost anything?

When it came time for the prayer part of our home visit with the squatting man. I volunteered to pray. I prayed a prayer reminding God, as if He needs reminding, of the lepers that His Son Jesus, healed. I prayed reminding God of the lame man who was let down through a hole that had been cut through the roof so he could be healed by His Son, Jesus. This was my new way of praying, not just words begging God for selfish desires, but praying with the faith of the walk that Jesus took. Amen.

About 6 months later, at home in Kentucky, I ran into one of the other missionaries that had been with me on "Uncle Tippy's" home visit. He had been back to Haiti since I had and he said, "Remember that man you prayed for that couldn't stand up? I saw him. He's standing tall and walking, just like you and I."

Voodoo In America

To me voodoo is anything that separates you from the Love of God and His desires for you to be the authentic person that He created you to be. To me addictions are a form of voodoo, people who are abusive to their families are under a form of voodoo, gangs are voodoo, cigarettes, racism, the desperate house wives, the Jersey Shores, Survivor, Sex in the City and the myriad of reality TV venues are a form of voodoo. I claim that worry, depression, suicide, murder--all voodoo. But when I share these thoughts people abruptly change the subject or try to explain to me that voodoo is a religion. True. Voodoo is a condition.

I visited an elementary school and shared about Haiti. I took some of my souvenirs with me to show the students. I had some small dolls that were hand made by the women of Haiti. They were supposedly voodoo dolls. Dolls that I had "rescued". One of the boys asked, as he quickly passed one of the dolls to the student next to him, "Do you believe in Voodoo Ms. Pace?" Ah great question, now was my chance.

"No I don't believe in voodoo. I believe in Jesus Christ as my Lord and Savior. I believe that God gave us all a mind. I believe that we are made in God's image and part of that reflection is that we have the power of choice. So if I wake up in the morning and say I got up on the wrong side of the bed, then I believe that all day long bad things will happen to me.

If I am having a great day, and someone says to me, "what's wrong Ms. Pace, you look like you aren't feeling well." Then I will begin to have aches and pains. If I look in the mirror in the morning and say, 'Oh no. I'm gonna have a bad hair day.' All day long I will fiddle-faddle and rearrange and fuss over my hair. So if you are asking me if I believe that if I took a strand of your hair and wrapped it around the neck of this doll, do I believe that it will make you fall in love with me? No, I don't believe that. But I do believe that Jesus is the Son of God and that He died on the cross as punishment for my sins and that He arose again defeating death on the 3rd day.

And because of this great act of Love I serve Him and make choices based on His great love for me. But no, son, I do not believe in voodoo."

CHAPTER THIRTY FIVE
FLASHBACKS: WHEN DID WE SEE THEE

And the Disciples Asked Jesus
"When did we see thee naked or hungry?"

Flashbacks of Haiti

I thought that I would have
sleepless nights as a missionary
But I sleep very well,
It's my daylight hours that are restless.
Instead of nightmares
I have daymares
flashbacks of Haiti.

The Whole Story

3 teachers

152 children

No books

No paper

No pencils

No crayons

No scissors

No posters on the wall

No alphabet or number cards

Just one ratty Teacher's binder

Full of yellowed

Crinkly edged papers

You Do The Math

I WAS FURIOUS. We were sending monies to the school to sponsor teachers. $1800, was suppose to cover a teacher's salary for a year, all of her supplies and books and one meal a day for each of her students. I saw none of this. I lit into one of the missionaries in charge.

"Where is our $1800 going?"

He informed me that "A teacher is fully sponsored only if ALL of the teachers are sponsored. Only 10 of 41 teachers are currently sponsored at this school. So the money for the 10 is divided amongst the 41. Yolantha, you do the math."

Oh how I wanted to give a real inner city snake bite reply, but I couldn't through the sting of holding back the tears that threatened to splash down the math side of my brain. It was so difficult at times not to allow the dragon breath of my past to incinerate and obliterate the insensitive obstacles that blocked my path and caused my heart to cringe. Oh God, America, we can do better than this."

And then when His time here was over, He encouraged His followers that they would do even greater and grander things than He.

CHAPTER THIRTY FIVE

Spitting Into The Ocean

Who do you think you are?
Oprah Winfrey?
What's the use
There is no excuse
For the degree of poverty I see
Compared to the abundance
of American opulence
I live
There's no way to rearrange
And affect change.
It's like spitting into the ocean
One tic-tac
No matter how strategically placed
Won't change the stench of a pile of cow manure
A scented candle won't mask the aroma of a skunk
A boy scout knife won't win a revolution
It's like spitting into the ocean.
Yet I return to Haiti once again,
my ancestral hope won't die…
It's tea dumping time!
I pass out a one quart baggy of rice
and a one quart baggy of beans
That is suppose to feed a blended family of 18,
one American meal at a time
But I leave the home visit
Knowing the Haitian mother

FLASHBACKS: WHEN DID WE SEE THEE

will time the meals
Stretching her one quart baggy of rice
and her one quart baggy of beans
for the family of 18 so it will feed them
for a full Haitian week.
And I spit and I spit and I spit
Does the ocean even notice?

Get An Education

Teechuh say
"Get an education."
Get an education
But din fo whut
So I will be abul to add?
Add the numbuh of deys since I last ate?
So I will be abul to subtract
The numbuh of babies from duh village
That died las mont
So I will be abul to conjugate death
I die
You die
He and she dies
Yesterday I died
Yesterday they died
Tomorrow we will all die
"but teechuh,
At this moment I am dying alive!"

Alive

I study my geography
And my social studies
And learn of people in other lands
That are fat with pride and
Wasteful with hope as they plan
Their day around the sounds of
Doing many little nothings
While I plan my day around sighing and dying.
How much education does it take teacher
To die with dignity?
Teacher,
What is the answer to the square root of
A life without food or clean water?
What is the equation with "X"
That will give me
A future?
To die with dignity is
My response
To any academic question
You can pose.
That is not just my educated guess
That is my final
Answer to Haiti.
Oh teechuh
How will you grade my ansuh?

Calling All African Americans

Later on, high on the mountain top
I was watching Eddie,
Our team leader
Play
With one of the little Haitian boys,
Laughing and tickling
And tussling and just enjoying life
A little while later,
I asked the little boy, again caught up
In my American arrogance,
"What do you want to be when you grow up?
This little sun baked, coal black boy thought for a while,
Grinning brightly at our team leader he ventured,
"I want to be a white man just like Eddie,"
That night I lay awake
Surrounded by my mosquito net
Listening to the mosquitoes sing.

Whazza Missionary to Do?

Before my first trip there had been only teams of men going to the mission field of Ranquitte. Up until the year 2000 the living conditions were considered too rough for us American women. Before the women, the male missionaries proudly adorned the naked children with Nike, Adidas, Wild Cats, Cowboys, Steelers, Chicago Cubs…tee-shirts. They didn't think to bring…underwear. After our first female team left in the year 2000 we made sure the following year, 2001, that we brought the children underwear…and girlie girl blouses for the girls. Since then, because of the vastness and grossness of the poverty, I've seen many of my daughter's blouses being worn by some of the boys. What's a missionary to do?

The Good Deed

We were building a Happy Haitian Home. The children from the village stood around naked and watched. We had brought clothes with us from America, but they were still neatly folded on the huge conference table in the front room of our missionary compound. I couldn't understand what we were waiting for? Why not distribute the clothes now to these children? At lunch time we went back and had a scrumptious meal. After getting permission from the other missionaries I stuffed a backpack full of clothes to take to the children and some granola bars, because I knew they were just sitting at the building site waiting for us to return from our scrumptious meal. They waited, naked, without any lunch.

We returned to the site. I passed out granola bars and clothes. We continued to build. Out of the corner of my eye I kept seeing a blue flurry of fighting movements. I turned to see what was the matter. There was a little boy wrestling with himself over his little blue shirt. The first shirt he had ever owned. I had graciously given him a shirt, but had ungraciously, not taught him how to put it on.

CHAPTER THIRTY SIX
"AHA"

I hurriedly scurried into church and tried to slip unnoticed into a pew. That day God strategically placed me in the balcony behind a stressed out mom and her rambunctious two year old son. He fiddled and wiggled and alternated between walking the pew and crawling on his belly like a reptile. He then delighted himself by repeatedly rolling back and forth under the pew until he started giggling profusely. The mother dug frantically through her purse, pulled out a baggy of cereal and desperately dangled the prize out over her lap. The little boy, made a bee line to his mother's lap and sat like an angel docilely popping the cereal one at a time into his mouth. I couldn't believe it was the same child.

AHA, AHA, AHA!!! CEREAL. Light weight, filling, you don't have to have fire to cook it. Perfect for Vacation Bible School snack for the children of Haiti and home visits. I could hear angels singing in the background. "Aaahaaaaaaaa"

When I shared the "aha" light bulb moment with my prayer partners they burst my spiritual high.

"You can't take cereal, they will need milk."

I was stumped. Milk never entered my mind.

I stammered, "I made it through college eating dry frosted flakes in the middle of the night." The raised eyebrows of my upper middle class American prayer warriors cut me to the quick. I went on to say, humbly reminded of my own personal poverty, "Mothers in America often feed their children dry cereal in public to keep them quiet."

"Cereal without milk?" I could see this was about socio-economics.

CHAPTER THIRTY SIX

I left the prayer session frustrated. I got into my 1998 used Dodge Caravan, slammed the door, looked into my rear view mirror and God said, "Man does not live by milk alone."

A week before I left for Haiti, my Sunday School class and prayer partners surprised me with a CEREAL PARTY. They filled the back of my 1998 used dodge Caravan with baggy after baggy after baggy of cereal. Bees came from miles around, drawn by the sweet aroma that embraced my ride.

CHAPTER THIRTY SEVEN
PERFECT

Perfect Haitian English

I looked up and 3young men
Were walking beside me
I would guess them to be 20 to 23 years of age
Even though they looked to be
Only 15 by American standards.
We would walk 20 steps
They would turn their heads,
Stare at me and smile
As we walked.
I'd look back at them and they would look away
We'd walk some more
Then before long they would stare again
I'd look at them and smile, they would quickly look away
And we'd walk some more.
After a while the silence bothered my Americanisms
I was compelled to start making polite conversation
I had long sense run out of things to say
Since I don't speak Creole
The young people always want to practice their English
But there are only so many
Hello, how are you, what is your name conversations
That one American can do in a day
I asked in my perfect American English,
"What would it take to fix Haiti? To make Haiti perfect"

CHAPTER THIRTY SEVEN

Without missing a beat,
One of the young men said,
In perfect
Haitian English
"Jesus"
We walked that last mile to the compound
Without staring, smiling or
Saying another word.

WATER WATER EVERYWHERE AND NOT A DROP TO DRINK

How Much Water Does It Take?

How much water do we use in America
To take a shower, take a bath or wash our car?
Imagine
My bath water, mop bucket water,
Standing toilet water, dish water…
Cleaner
Than the water available to the mountain children of Haiti.
Until you see a child dying of dehydration
Hear the moans and groans of a child
Crying without tears…
Pouring the water off of a pot of spaghetti
Down the kitchen sink
Would never give you a second thought.
But I've seen and
I've heard..
I've stood motionless for 45 minutes…
Staring at the sink
Where I watched
My spaghetti water disappear,
Wondering…
How many children…
Just my spaghetti water alone…
Could save.

Our Water Bearer

He proudly and carefully carries buckets dancing with
Clear, clean hand washing water
For the missionaries
And drinking water
For the missionaries
And shower water
for the missionaries
Knowing that his own family
Washes and drinks and brushes their teeth
In the same water in which his donkey drinks.
He quickly repents
Thanking God he even owns a donkey
A purchase he was able to make
With the money he gets from fetching
Clear, clean hand washing water
For the missionaries
And drinking water for the missionaries
And shower water
For the missionaries
His mind once again wanders
Would his dying baby girl improve
If she could only just even sip
The used missionary bath water
Instead of the same water in which
His donkey drinks.

WATER WATER EVERYWHERE

The Wells Are Dry

Ronald's baby sister has not laughed for 10 days. She is sick and needs water badly. Ronald's mother sends him to fetch water. The water well is nearly a mile away. Ronald runs because he loves his mother and is obedient. Ronald runs because he adores his baby sister and loves to hear her laugh. Ronald arrives at the well in good time. But there is a crowd of children around the well with empty buckets. The well is dry. Ronald knows the next well is a half mile away and has been dry now for over 2 months and the one after that has bad water. The next after that is 3 miles away. He imagines he hears his sister's laughter and runs like the wind the 3 miles. It will take him longer to return in order not to waste any of his sister's precious water. As he nears the well he sees children kicking up dust and swinging empty buckets. One of the boys says the well is empty and the missionaries aren't coming again to fix it for another month. Ronald swallows with a parched throat and hurries the 4 miles back to his mother. He gets to the edge of his yard. His heart hears the angelic sound of his sister's laughter. He hurriedly enters his inadequate hut made of mud, sticks, and banana leaves. His mother rocks his sister tightly to her body. She rocks humming a deep sound that smells of the ancestors. She rocks to and fro, fro and to.

"The wells are dry," says Ronald. He leans over swaying to his mother's rhythm and kisses his baby sister. She is sleeping with a smile. Her skin is cool like fresh water after the rain. "My friends say that the missionaries are coming to the wells in a month.

CHAPTER THIRTY EIGHT

"It doesn't matter now," responds his mother, still gently rocking his baby sister to and fro, fro and to.

Ronald goes out into his yard and squats down to cry. His body is so thirsty from all of the days effort that his eyes won't waste the water.

CHAPTER THIRTY NINE
THE ROADS

A Good Bright Sun Shiny Day

The roads.
They are so bad that it can take
Any where from 2 to 3 hours to
Make the 12 mile distance from
The airport in Pignon to the
Missionary compound outside of Ranquitte
And that's on a good, bright sun shiny day
If it has rained or is raining it takes exceedingly longer
The ruts in the roads can get as high as my knees
And I am a tall woman, standing 5 feet 9 and ½ inches.
That's a 20 inch deep pothole
It can be so wide that it takes up the whole road
One day I walked the 12 miles distance
From Ranquitte to the Pignon airfield
It took me 2 hours and 17 minutes
Just 2 minutes longer that day than the truck ride
It was a good, bright, sun shiny day.

"You can't save the world..."

CHAPTER FOURTY
WHAT DO YOU DO?

Crackers and Cookies

We came to a home with many children. We tried to visit with the mother but the children kept scrambling, running in and around, poking, pecking and distracting mama. I foraged around in my missionary pockets and found 4 cookies and 6 crackers. The children became so calm and sedate a huge hush captured the household. I rambled on saying missionary type things, doing the usual survey type questions. When it came time to leave we did our usual spiel about offering to pray with the family.

"Are there any special prayer requests?" I asked in my redundant manner not anticipating what came next.

The mother looked at me, gazing into the inner sanctums of my core in the way that only a mother can tap into another mother, touching the birth canal depths of the matriarchal soul. Our translator translated to me her response.

"I want to know your God of the cookies and the crackers."

Stunned, I offered her the Plan of Salvation. She, without hesitation, accepted Jesus Christ as her personal Lord and Savior.

It should have been a joyous occasion for me yet I left full of anguish and fire because the God I serve is larger than 4 cookies and 6 crackers. I've got to do better.

5 years later--and still I step forth and offer a God of a hand full of crackers and some cookie crumbs. I know that God is not a liar. Could it be that I am the falsehood of His Kingdom? And it hurts

sooooo very, very bad. I need help. My cry becomes--"Help me to feed and provide clean water and education for just 200 children and their families in the remote mountain area of Ranquitte, Haiti."

"Yolantha, you can't save the world."

And I want to shout, "but, but, but…I don't want to save the world, I just want one small village community of approximately 200 children. I want those 200 children healthy, clean and smart. And from the ranks of that 200 children may come the answer to the poverty of Haiti, the answer to social reform, the answer to the horrendous road systems, or the cure for cancer or the answer to cerebral palsy, muscular dystrophy or Alzheimer's."

Why 200? That is the number God gave me, and from within that 200 may come the boy or girl who creates and implements strategies for peace throughout the world. It still after 10 years reverberates in my heart.

"I want to know your God of cookies and crackers."

What Do You Do?

American woman
What do you do when
Your breasts are empty of milk
And dere is no grocery
And de baby don cry
Cause tears take water
And de well is dry
For 2 months now
Death eats our children with a bow
American woman
What do you do?

"How many Bibles do you have?"

CHAPTER FOURTY ONE
TWO BIBLES

The Protocol

1. Get permission to come on property
2. Ask the survey questions
3. Give medical attention if there is a medic present
4. Pass out supplies
5. Pray

Changing The Protocol

From past experiences in America, I never liked when church folk made the homeless listen to a long sermon before feeding them. People can't hear when their stomachs are so loud with hunger. One year God convicted me to change the protocol Now my protocol is

1. Get permission to come on the property
2. Immediately pass out supplies, asking them if I can give them some rice and beans and clothes on behalf of our Lord and Savior Jesus Christ. I tell them that I have not gold or silver but what I have I want to in the name of my Lord and Savior, Jesus Christ, give freely.
3. Give medical attention if there is a medic present
4. Ask the survey questions
5. Pray

Feed the people first…IT'S A GOD THANG.

CHAPTER FORTY ONE

Two Bibles

One year God provided Bibles for us to pass out during home visits. I was ecstatic! That year we also had an African American man who was on his first ever missionary trip. I was ecstatic! On home visits we divide into teams. We divided into 3 teams of 4. My African America brother and I were on different teams. I was ecstatic!

"Please suh, may I have another Bible for my wife who is at the market?" The Haitian husband asked the male African American Missionary.

The male African American's Missionary team had run out of Bibles. The African American Missionary said to the Haitian husband, brother to brother, man to man, "I will get you another Bible." The other European American Missionaries overheard the request and the African American Missionary's response.

"No! One Bible per family." Said the White Missionary.

When my team joined the other teams at the truck in order to return to the compound, the African American missionary pulled me aside. He explained to me the situation and expressed his deep pain because he had given his word, "brother to brother, man to man." The third team of missionaries joined us at the truck. They had some Bibles they did not get to distribute. I grabbed one of the extra Bibles and began to walk back up the path accompanied by my missionary soul brother. One of the other missionaries admonished us.

"If we give out more than one Bible to a family then we won't have enough to go around."

TWO BIBLES

Something about the tone of voice hit my spiritual nerve. I turned with the wrath of Jesus in the Temple.

"How many Bibles do you have at your home in America? I'm only guessing, but I am embarrassed to say, I'm sure I have at least 12 and I for sure have not read the Bible 12 times through. And I'm ashamed to say I've barely even read one of them from cover to cover."

I proceeded up the hill with my brother of color who was also my dear brother in Christ . Off we went to the very gracious and beholding man who just wanted a Bible for his wife. I can still hear more than 4 years later his "merci" (thank you) ringing in my ears and see the crinkle of love for his wife in the corners of his eyes.

When we returned to the truck, one of the missionaries hissed, "How do you know that he isn't just going to sell the other Bible for money?"

I didn't think to pray. Forgive me Jesus, I pounded my fist in the palm of my hand. I hissed back, "Then he, his wife and his family will eat!"

Help me Jesus, I need prayer.

Happy Haitian Homes

I helped build a Happy Haitian Home. Upon the completion of the home I asked if we ever went back to pray with and visit the families after we built their homes. I was told that we usually do one follow up visit 6 months to a year later to check on the construction.

"So we document the status of the building but we don't document the well-being of the family for which the building was built?"

No response.

I decided to tag along for one of the annual revisit inspections. We knocked on the door of one of our Happy Haitian Homes from the past. Only the houses in the mountains that we Americans build have the luxury of a door. After what seemed like a long while the residents came out and stood in front of the house. I wondered how often they had visitors who came and knocked on their door. The missionary inspectors snapped pictures. Strangely the Happy Haitian home owners looked just like the same starving and famished family that stood in front of their original lean-to of a home made of sticks and mud and banana leaves.

To my naïve amazement, concrete floors, American walls and a permanent weather proof roof do not a Happy Haitian make.

Happy Haitian Hearts

Not only are they famished for food
But hey are starving for the joy of Jesus
We bring physical construction
But we neglect the spiritual resurrection
We are building homes without a foundation of hope
We have all the supplies we need
But the wrong parts
We are lacking the materials that matter.
We sweat hard and I worry that
The new houses we build will never become homes
For lack of biblical instruction
And the tools for constructing
Happy Haitian souls
That turn into
Happy Haitian Hearts
That reside in
Happy Haitian homes.

"Now they will have hope..."

CHAPTER FOURTY TWO
OH NO, NOT AGAIN!

There It Was Again

"**M**ix Youlanda," the principal of the school beamed, "you are here, the childrun are berry, berry happy. Now they will have hope."

There it was again. The people of Haiti are linking me with their hope. This is difficult for me because I was always taught that my hope is in Jesus Christ and whenever I've misplaced or displaced that hope I have been mightily disappointed.

The voice of the Lord said, "Yolantha you are using me as an excuse not to do marvelous things. Yolantha, my hope also rests in you."

My stomach flopped and cuss words churned around in the depths of my gut as I was bombarded by the many times I had hopelessly disappointed the Lord.

"The call is

The invitation to work with the doing power of God"

CHAPTER FOURTY THREE
WHO ME?

Every time I returned home to my America, I took stock of my intentions and did spiritual inventory.

There Needs to Be

CALLING 101-THE GREAT COMMISSION: a basic introductory class for new Christians; recognizing, defining, embracing and empowering the call; final exam--7 days on the mission field. (this class cannot be audited)

When I'm Honest With Myself

I have missed calls
I have sat by the phone
Screening my caller ID
Just watching the phone ring,
I have observed others answering the call
Even though I was closer to the call
I have even unplugged the phone
So as not to be bothered by calls
And when I'm honest with myself…
I have tragically treated the call of God the same.

The Doing

The call is simple.
The call is
The invitation to work with the doing power of God
God is love and love is doing
Feelings and emotions
Are not love
They are the by products of love
Not the validation for love
Nor the substantiation of love
God's love power
Creates
Blooms
Embarks seasons
Launches rainbows and ocean waves
Dies to itself
Births
Shares
Heals
Feeds
Nurses
Sacrifices.
Encourages
Builds
This is the call
The call to doing love.

CHAPTER FORTY THREE

The Call to Do What?

The call to do what?...Love

Yup, uh-huhn. Well that's vague. A long, long silence ensued.

Sorry that wasn't very respectful. Forgive me for being rude.

God is love

Duh-uh---forgive me Lord, but I know that. That's the second Bible verse I learned as a child, after Jesus wept.

That's love too.

What?

To love so much, to have so much compassion that you cry over what you see. Not just the physical state of things, but the spiritual and emotional emaciation throughout the world. Many teach that I cried over the physical loss of my dear cousin Lazarus. I could easily fix Lazarus, my cousin's death situation, but I cried over the accusatory tones of my friends and family for my late arrival. It is very rarely taught that I cried because I could do absolutely nothing about Martha and Mary's unbelief.

You know I was raised to believe that only sissies cry.

Yes, I know. In other words are you telling me that I, Jesus, the Son of God, am a sissy over you? Wouldn't it be awesome if your belief about me was as strong as your belief about crying being for sissies. Or your belief and dependence on gravity and the theory of relativity or Murphy's law. You wouldn't be half bad, Yolantha, if you had just as much trust in Me as you have trust in that chair you're sitting in to hold you up.

A long, long, long, silence...this time from me.

CIA

Stop being secret service Christians
I sent Jesus my son
I sent Him out into the open
The great commission is the call for all CIA:
CHRISTIANS IN ACTION
It's a call to go
Not observe
Not supervise
Not critique.
It's a call to making
Not pontificating
It's not about making excuses of why you can't
But it's about making excuses of why you can
Because the day is gonna come for each and every one
When you will have to explain
Why you didn't do the right thing as well as
Why you did.

You a Lie!

Surely you aren't talking to me
Surely not me
If you had told me as a child
That I would grow up to be a missionary
I would probably have said
"You a lie"
And stormed out of the room.
Even today, after 10 years
On the foreign mission field
I still often can't believe it
And want to storm out of the room.

CHAPTER FOURTY FOUR
IT'S PERSONAL

God Calls Louder

I'm disemboweled
no matter how much
I try
To stuff me back inside
Another fragile organ plops
Out
I try
Keeping silent,
I try looking the other way
I try not getting involved
But then
Children lack
Run away and
Never come back
I try
Not to take you or me or them so seriously
When I try those tries
Children starve
Children cry
Children die.

Extreme Love Makeover

In the
Garden of
Gethsemane
The decision to give
The decision to go
The decision to stay
And
The decision to be crucified
That…
Is love,
Ultimate love,
Extreme love.

The Task, My Covenant, It's Personal

Yolantha
Go,
Tell,
Baptize and
Disciple!
Pitting your God against
Any god that man will challenge you with
The god of criticism and alienation
The god of self medication
The god of drunken stupors
And unfounded rumors
The god of over eating and self defeating
The god of darkness and fear of night
The god of negligence and oversight
The god of exhaustion and worry
The god of slow down what's the hurry
The god of doubt and being without
The god of no you can't go
Tell them to bring their gods
If they dare
Then step behind me
As God above I promise uncensored love
Yolantha, I care and
It's...
Personal.

I'm Excited

There is anticipation of
What my flesh can handle or understand
There is anticipation
At the knowledge of my past failures
God overrides
"I know, Yolantha, I know."
I bless you through your failures
So that I,
God,
Might succeed
It's my turn now.
Go forth and multiply
Using the special equipping testimony tools of your life."
I'm excited.

The Proposal

Do you, Yolantha,
take God Almighty
to be your spiritually wedded God?
I do.
(What next?)

Guerilla Warfare

"**Y**es, Lord Jesus. I'll go!"
Excitement poured all over me
And clung to me like expensive perfume.
"Yeeeeeeehaaaaaaw!"
My innards, hip-hopped, waltzed and promenaded
Trying to tame my childlike heart

Once I said yes, I thought folks would be overjoyed and support-ive. But quite the contrary, folks thought I was plum crazy. Some were supportive of my call to missionary work, but thought that I was a lunatic to even consider going to Haiti. I even had 2 "celebrity types" in the African American community admonish me for going to Haiti.

"We go to Africa" the television actress announced boldly.

"Why?" I asked, "Haiti is so much closer."

"It's too dangerous. There is a certain longitude and latitude quadrant that Americans aren't encouraged to travel within, because of the risk factor. Haiti falls in that quadrant."

"What risk factor?"

"Haiti is unpredictable and doesn't play by America's rules." She then laughed. "If they kidnapped you, we have no bargaining chips by which to get you back." She had a point, but then I thought sadly that the only African Americans that America would pay a ran-som for is Oprah and Obama. So I wasn't really worth kidnapping.

Kentucky folks asked, "Ain't you skeered?" nodding their heads in that yes way that I learned as a convincing strategy in business when you want an opponent to agree with you or a potential client to make a purchase from you.

Well I wasn't "skeered". But this ain't the first time I was too ignorant to know to be afraid.

Business As Usual

Now that I've said yes,
Every…Every…
Every thing has
Tilted off of its axis.
Nothing
is in balance
What's happening to me?
Every thing
is off.
I can't find a norm.
A place to chill out.
Everything
is on display
Everything
is under the microscope.
My eyes
are bugged out like frog's,
watching
My ears
are drooped like elephant's,
hearing
But they hone in
like the sonar radar of a bat,
listening,
It's nothing I can place my finger on
Yet when I touch things

IT'S PERSONAL

Their textures burn
Past my known layer of skin.
I feel things
beneath a deeper within.
Something
is about to happen.
The gun is lifted,
the flags are raised,
The engines are revving
The horses are pressed
hard against the gate.
Volcanic energy
is exploding in my womb
Yet I am compelled
to walk around
Pretending
that everything is
'business as usual.'

What Am I Made Of?

Since saying yes
Satan tries me and challenges me to see
What I am made of.
Since saying yes,
I've lost my 5 bedroom 3 full bath home.
God quickly provided me a new home.
Since saying yes
I've been in 3 car wrecks.
2 cars were totaled
One accident sent
The person in front of me
And the person behind me to the hospital
Yet I was totally unscathed.
Each time
God quickly provided me with new transportation.
Since saying yes,

It's Personal

One year I had personally saved all of the finances needed for my trip to Haiti. Christmas Eve of Christmas Eve, December 23rd,...there was a knock on my door. I opened the door and there stood two policemen in full uniform regalia, their palms casually resting on their weapons. They asked for my husband and escorted him to jail. It took all of my Christmas shopping money and Haiti savings to get my husband back so he'd be home on Jesus' birthday. God quickly provided sponsors that year for me to do His work.

Since saying yes,

My husband got fired from his professorship and he has never recovered. God helped me to quickly find work.

Since saying yes

My father-in-law died a week before I was to leave for Haiti. Nobody told me until 8 hours before I was to board my plane. God quickly comforted me and said, "get on the airplane, let the dead bury the dead, I have a village full of living children waiting for us."

Since saying yes,

In 2008 I got banned from traveling with the organization I had been traveling with for 7 years. After a one year hiatus, God provided ways for me to travel independently in order to continue to do His work.

Now I focus on a new yes.

The "yes" of God. Which is probably the focus I should have had all along.

Soaring

Accepting the plight of a Christian's heart
This Jesus addiction feels so exasperatingly good.
Is this what every crack and heroin addict is chasing after?
There is this relief of joy
As each challenge is rewarded
With a promise
As I come out of hibernation
And rise higher,
Buffeted by the Holy Spirit wind as I morph
From caterpillar to butterfly to
Eagle rising
Soaring

God's Promise to An Obedient Woman…
It's Personal

II DEUTERONOMY 15:9

Yolantha,

If the poor cry out to God against you for not meeting their need, then you have sinned.

II DEUTERONOMY 15:10

Yolantha

Don't give to the poor with a grieved heart. My Deuteronomy promise to you, Yolantha, is that I, God, will bless you in all your words and in all that you put your hand on.

I will honor whatever you do or give to the poor, Everything else you do, everything else you touch, will be blessed.

And I am going to take it a step further.

Likewise anyone who takes mercy on you and your family and assists you in the work that I am doing through you,

> They too,
> I WILL BLESS.
> It's personal.

"Help me Holy Spirit..."

Chapter Fourty Five
QUESTIONING THE CALL

Mathew Seven Seven

I must be asking the wrong question
I already know the right answer
The answer is
"...feed the children, give the children clean water to drink
Give them hope of a life with dignity, show them Jesus."
I was recently told that I wasn't asking the wrong questions
But that I was asking the wrong people.
When you witness what I witness there are no "wrong people"
Authentic people, "real people"
Feed their children, provide education,
show love, goodness and mercy
And uplift their children.
So it's got to be a fallacy in my question
Not the people.
So I've changed it from
Will you make a donation
Which non-authentic people can't seem to hear
To "how's your day today?"
But I'd just as soon be asking
"how now, brown, cow?"
Help me holy spirit
To just ask!
Matthew 7:7--

"Ask, and it shall be given to you, seek and you shall find; knock, and it shall be opened to you."

Matthew 7:8

"for everyone who asks receives, and he who seeks finds. And to him who knocks it shall be opened. Or what man is there among you, when his son shall ask him for a loaf, will give him a stone? Or if he shall ask for a fish he will not give him a snake, will he? If you then, being evil, know how to give good gifts to your children, how much more shall your Father who is in heaven give what is good to those who ask Him! There fore, however you want people to treat you, so treat them, for this is the Law and the Prophets."

An Email from Haiti

My Dearest and Sweetest Yolantha,

It is so good to hear from you. I am more than happy to hear that God gives you a chance to come to Ranquitte in June. Hopefully He will provide you all that you need to come. You are more than wanted in Ranquitte. We love you exceedingly. I cannot control my joy because you tell me that you are coming. We will have a wonderful moment with your beloved kids. Let me tell you something. In February a group of people came to do Vacation Bible School. I was with them.

All the kids kept on asking for you because they didn't feed them. You can imagine how important you are for them. Your presence is more than necessary and important. Hope to hear from you before long. We love you a lot. You are even too dear for me and my family, we love and appreciate you the most. Remember me to your children.

Your incomparable friend
God bless and provide for your needs.
François,
Your translator

Dashboard Reality

I am stripped naked,
Very vulnerable
A missionary
Standing toe to toe with Satan
And his religiosity

Dashboard Response

Naked you came into the world
Naked I am sending you out
No crutches, no security blankets, no rabbit's foot
Just you and My Word...
You do have enough of My Word to cover you don't you?
Don't you?
Have you studied enough
To show yourself...
Approved?

Living The Call

Before Haiti
The GREAT COMMISSION was
An obvious non-tangible.
Stuff done by preachers and missionaries
Big Godly stuff
In the pulpit and
Way off some where.
Kinda like the U.S. constitution is
A document only truly understood
By presidents, senators, governors and politicians…
However…as an American
The Constitution is the foundation for my rights
As a citizen of the United States.
Likewise as a Christian,
The GREAT COMMISSION
Is the foundation for my rights
As a citizen of the heavenly kingdom.

Forever Calling

God warns
"I am forever calling you,
Yet you tune me out,
Or you have hearing of selectivity."
God cautions
"I will cause the voice of exaltation to cease
And the voice of rejoicing to leave the land."
God has been true to His word
But often I am false to mine
Oh God, have mercy.

Spiritual Flaws

This is my struggle: Granted the missionaries have done and are doing a great and marvelous thing in Haiti, but sometimes I wonder what am I doing and sacrificing for? Is it because of the love that Jesus showed me by dying on the cross? Is it my struggle for some sort of deep seeded need for approval or spiritual feather in my cap? Or does my spirituality center around alleviating guilt over horrendous secret sins I've committed? I have to wonder often about our motives. My motives. I am deeply aware of my character flaws, but recognizing and addressing my spiritual flaws, well that's a completely different thing. One of my spiritual flaws that I can't seem to shake is "My Americanisms." One of which, that haunts me the most in Haiti is that I can't seem to shake that as an American I am "entitled" to be able to live a life of dignity. Who or what defines that entitlement, the right? Who or what defines "a life of dignity"?

Dignity

Many of my secret sins against God have evolved around the definition of "a life of dignity". I grew up thinking that it was not dignified to be single, eating in restaurants alone, going to movies alone. So I dated and got married in order to be perceived as a woman of dignity, in spite of the multitudes of undignified things that went on as a result of those "dignifying" relationships. My lack of social graces with white women often stemmed around them making me feel less than what I was worth. Meaning that to me, they were stealing, trampling or spitting upon my sense of dignity. Even the abortions in my life were agonizingly rationalized around my lack of ability to give a child a life of dignity and grace. However, the bulk of the agony was the lack of dignity resulting in facing my family with the generational curse of not being married and announcing, "I'm pregnant." Secret sins are often shielded with invisible umbrellas defined as good works. Umbrellas that distract us and shield us from the healing stripes and the forgiving covering of the crucified blood of Christ.

In spite of the numerous sermons that teach us that we cannot work out our salvation I meet and work with a multitude of missionaries like me that seem to be trading in their salvation trying to work out their sins. This trade off causes us to limp toward the finish line. It causes us to miss the boat of empowering miracles. It causes us to minimize the power of faith, because our secret sins seem so immensely unforgivable. We cannot fathom that God can forgive what we ourselves cannot or we ourselves will not.

"The question of dignity..."

CHAPTER FOURTY SIX
IT MUSTA BEEN THE HEAT

After a long strenuous steamy day on the mission field we traditionally wind down with an evening of devotionals. We talk about the high lights and low lights of the day; the victories and the challenges. This particular journey something was sticking in my craw that I could no longer ignore.

I raised the question of dignity…the fact that we have school children urinating and defecating under a tree outside the window of their classroom…in plain view of the other students. This was extremely bothersome to me. (Perhaps because as a child growing up we were made to stay outside all day long. We weren't allowed to come inside and use the bathroom. We had to use the bathroom on the side of the house. I remembered how humiliating it felt to bare my behind outside and squat to do such private and personal things. I was always afraid that the neighbors could see me or someone would round the corner of the house and catch me in the act.)

The other missionaries didn't bat an eye. They just giggled and smiled and spoke to me in that pious "there-there, it's okay tone" that I detested.

"They are used to it. While we are on the work site, it's not at all unusual to see a grown man step off to the side and relieve himself. That's what they are used to, it's just what they do."

It musta been the heat. I became furious. All I could think was that as a child what my brothers and I did on the side of the house was what we "had" to do. I NEVER GOT USED TO IT. I had to remind myself that most of the missionaries I traveled with are upper middle class to upper high class on the American socio-economic scale. They owned businesses, flew airplanes, vacationed the world. They did not struggle for every penny to get to Haiti the way that I did. They probably never ever HAD to use the bathroom outside on a regular basis or as part of their daily routine.

It musta been the hot Haitian heat. I most definitely had to have had a mild case of sun stroke because images of the indignities and indecencies of American slave life cascaded before me. It musta been the hot Haitian heat that reminded me how long slavery lasted and that it was followed by the lingering legacies instilled by the pseudo legalities of Jim Crowism. It musta been the hot Haitian heat that caused my skin to crawl with the non-tangibles of institutional-ized racism and the vast amount of African American illiteracy that still stains my country. It musta been the hot Haitian heat that made me not buy the fact that all of this notorious history was contingent upon America's Eurocentric assumption of "that's what THEY are used to." I may be used to eating spam, but that doesn't mean I shouldn't have access to steak.

For some reason on this particular sweltering day I just couldn't leave well enough alone. That one statement, "That's what THEY are used to"...set me on edge, it was the preverbal straw that broke my camel's back. I truly lost control. My deep ancestral roots, call it PMS, call it my sense of racial pride; compelled me to bring up the health clinic. I asked what I thought started out as a "non-threatening" question.

"How are things going at the clinic?" It got very quiet.

"Our board of directors runs things regarding the clinic."

The tone of voice made me feel as if I was being scolded this time for questioning the powers that be. I recognized the feeling in the pit of my stomach of rancid lava boiling up ready to spew at any moment. I am old enough and cross generational enough to recog-nize the ancestral feelings that overtook the atmosphere. A tone of voice I saw used when I was a little girl in elementary school in the early 1960's of "needing to be put in my place for speaking out of turn as a colored gal". The early memory began to permeate and goose pimple my flesh.

It musta been the Haitian heat for something wouldn't let go of me and somebody's voice (it sounded vaguely like mine) addressed the male missionary. "If your wife was ill would you send your wife to our clinic? Some of you know and have spent time with my daughter Diamond. Would you feel comfortable sending her to our clinic?" Their silence caused me to truly step over the "line". Once I lost control of that interracial censoring mechanism I couldn't gage when enough was enough.

"And what about these Happy Haitian Homes we've been building? Why are they all the same size for a family of 4 as a family of 7 and a family of 18? Why don't we make them in small, medium, and large like we do in America with our Habitats for Humanity?"

Then came the retaliation that clearly drew the dividing line.

"Are you questioning why we are here; what we are doing? We are doing the best that we can. At least it's better than nothing."

Kaboom!!! My insides exploded. My insides shouted, "What proverb…what scripture is that? What part of the great commission encompasses that attitude?"

A voice said very quietly, calmly and with a matter of fact, "And we call ourselves Christians? If this is the best we can do as Christians, I don't wanna be a Christian."

I couldn't believe that somebody had spoken the very thing that I was thinking out loud. I looked around at the missionaries to see who had spoken my very thoughts. I was shocked to see that each missionary was staring at me. That calm, quiet, matter of fact voice, was mine.

Then all of sudden I felt a POOF! That feeling of dismissal that White Americans are good at doing. That small gush of wind that immediately exiles undesirables into the land of invisibility. I had been "dismissed"; no longer worthy of consideration.

The subject was immediately changed to something as banal as the price of tea in China or some such non threatening religious tête-à-tête. I was being ignored like a recalcitrant child who just didn't now any better.

We closed the meeting with sounds that represented prayer. I walked my INVISIBLE self outside onto the porch. It was raining. Raining hard in the deep of the darkness of the stifling hot night. Praise God for the rain. I wept and my tears with the moisture from heaven plummeted simultaneously staining the Haitian earth.

I stood in the rain and I cried like I had never cried before. Perhaps much like Jesus wept after the death of His cousin Lazarus. I cried as Christ cried, not for the loss of Lazarus, but for Martha and Mary and the unbelief of the people . I found that I was weeping, not for Haiti, but for us as missionaries. I was crying for the limitations that we place on God.

Then a phenomenal thing occurred. It was if I was transported to the Garden of Gethsemane.

A voice said, "Daddy, I turned water into wine. I matched wits and stood toe to toe with the Pharisees and Sadducees. I restored dignity to the lowest of the low and offered a different path to the highest of the high, the richest of the rich. I fed thousands with baskets of food left to spare. I healed lepers. I cast out demons. So Father, I have done the best I can do, why should I have to go to the cross? I cleaned out Your temple. I raised folks from the dead...at least that's better than nothing. I've done the best I can do, Daddy, what more do you want?...so why the cross?...please Father...not the cross... but what about my dignity?...the cross?...I'm begging that if it be your will please, Papa, take this cup away from me...Father...Dad? ....Daddy?.....Oh God, Daddeeeee?"

I wept harder.

My tears brought me into submission and conviction. What if Jesus had snidely told His Father, "I've done the best I can do, Father, at least it's better than nothing," then got up off of his knees and rounded up his friends and left the Garden of Gethsemane through the back gate?

Not only didn't Jesus deserve to go to the cross; He had a choice, based on the life He had lived. He had lived and earned the right not to have to suffer the humiliation of such a horrific and demeaning death as THE CRUCIFIXION.

The rain, the heat and I became one. Am I doing the best that I can do?

Another Spiritual Flaw

My passion without compassion is a dangerous tool.

Defining

Having anything less in any venue of life than what God would want for us to have.

"Be angry, but sin not..."

CHAPTER FOURTY SEVEN
THE NATIVES ARE RESTLESS

I was born in 1955.

I grew up on black and white TV. I remember manually changing TV channels (a pair of pliers due to a lost TV knob), and foiled wrapped around the TV antennae as embellishment (a necessity for receiving a clear station and alleviating static). I grew up with Amos and Andy, I Love Lucy, Ed Sullivan, Baby Huey, Casper the Friendly Ghost, Walter Cronkite, Dr. Kildare, Maverick and Gunsmoke. The closest thing I had to MTV was Lawrence Welk and Mitch Miller. My favorite show of all time--Tarzan with the original Johnny Weissmuller.

The first time I saw people on TV that looked like me was on episodes of Tarzan. I adored the concept. Tarzan had been traveling with his parents as an infant when their plane crashed into the thick jungles of Africa. The whole premise is that the monkeys and apes found the infant and raised him as one of their own, teaching him how to survive in the jungle.

Every Saturday the plot revolved around white people coming to the jungles of Africa on a treasure hunting safari. They came exploiting the resources of the land for their own personal gain. Tarzan, friend to the villagers as well as the animals, was Africa's self appointed protector. The script writers' plot portrayed Tarzan's foes with a poaching mentality that centered around abusing, killing or destroying whole villages of African people in order to get the bounty that they desired. Saturday after Saturday, the white men would upset the balance of the Jungle and they would often raid and destroy everything in their path. The villagers of course responded as any patriot would in protection of his or her home land--with anger and a sense of vindication. The European response to the African's preparations for retaliation was summed up by the shows writers in one huge biting phrase that rolled weekly off the lips of the white intruders:

"The natives are getting restless!"

Even as a child that phrase 'the natives are getting restless' would agitate me because it was always the precursor to mass destruction of people who looked just like me. There was something in the way that it was said that made me feel subhuman. I couldn't understand as a child why I was expected to "let" the white man, or any person for that matter destroy my beautiful jungles, kill thousands of my elephants for their tusks, rape my land of her diamonds and me not respond. On Saturdays I was being indoctrinated into sitting idly by and watching these atrocities and indignities occur to the Great African Motherland. And I was being institutionally taught that the only person who could effectively "SAVE THE DAY" was a White man. As harsh as this sounds, the reality was that there were no African or African American hero counterparts to help "BALANCE THE DAY."

It was the last day of Vacation Bible School. We were preparing to hand out goody bags to slightly over 200 children who were waiting with hunger and excitement. The children began to push and shove in anticipation for their little packages. Somehow, the spirit of the children frightened the other female missionaries. They became nervous as the children began to push and shove and inch in toward them invading their personal space.

The women started gathering their skirts closer to themselves. They seemed to do what we as kids did when we played "COWBOYS" and the "INDIANS" were attacking us. Us "COWBOYS" would "circle up"; standing back to back as a strategy portraying unified strength against the "INDIANS". Then one of the missionaries said it. The phrase that I hadn't heard since I was 10 years old. The missionary clapped her hands at me, the way my mother used to clap her hands at our pet cocker spaniel when she was demanding its obedience.

"Hurry up,(clap-clap-clap) Yolantha, (clap-clap-clap) hurry up!!! (clap-clap-clap) The natives are getting restless. (clap)"

Suddenly out of nowhere my ancestral slave side stood face to face with my radical...say it loud I'm black and I'm proud side of the 1960's. My head snapped, my chest protruded, my legs went into straddle and I felt my feet grab earth. I was ready to fight, big time.

Out of the corner of my ear I heard, "Miss Yolantha, Miss Yolantha, me first, me first, me...me...me." Which snapped me back into reality. The venom and bile spit in my mouth splashed back down my throat replaced by a more cinnamon nurturing taste. I quickly began passing out bag after bag of wonderful goodies that had been prepared for the delight of the children--pencils, coloring books, toothbrushes, matchbox cars, afro picks, children's books with bright colored pictures, starlight mints, juicy-fruit chewing gum, baggies of Chex Party Mix. Angelic laughter and Holy Ghost glee was everywhere.

Later on that evening back at the missionary compound, sitting on the porch veranda the female missionaries were discussing their insights on the results of our day. I kept hearing phrases that included, "them" and "those people". The missionary that had clapped at me earlier, leaned over with her forearms on her lap, fanned herself in the hot Haitian evening with the edge of her skirt, and announced with a nervous giggle, "The natives sure were restless."

My flesh side forgot that my trigger was still cocked from earlier usage of this phrase. My insides went off like a double barrel shot gun.

Somebody, which I soon learned was me, said, "I'm not sure when we get back to America we will all be telling the same story about what we participated in today." I knew it had to have been me who said it cause all the other missionaries were glaring at me with their mouths open as if they were singing the last note of a church choir anthem.

That night laying in bed, unable to go to sleep I tried to recount what happened next on the porch. Phrases bombarded and ricocheted around in my head like in some Spike Lee horror movie.

"I don't know what you mean?"

"Are you saying that I'm a racist?"

"I went to school with a black person!"

"One of my best friends at work is black!"

I just couldn't figure the turn of events out. By the time our "discussion" ended a bucket of crocodile tears had been spilled and I was left sitting on the porch all alone. The only other thing that I remember saying that contributed to this onslaught of American anxiety was, "But why would anyone use the phrase, 'the natives are restless'? This isn't some Tarzan movie. Why do we keep saying 'them' and 'those people'? Because...but for the grace of God go you and I or your children and my children."

To my dismay there are now a host of women who will not go on the mission field if they know that I'm going. I fear that when I die, this will be one of those "be angry and sin not" scenarios that God will find it necessary to hold me accountable for.

CHAPTER FOURTY EIGHT
WHAT'S IT LIKE?

I'm asked often what it's like being at times the only Black Missionary with all White Missionaries?

Most of the time
I don't have the vocabulary
It is awesome no matter how I look at it
All senses are turned up several notches
My weaknesses confront my strengths
Often we live at different spots on America's time line
Based on our experiences in the realm of diversity
God shows me just what I am made of,
Something He already knows
But something about which most of the time
I have no clue.
What's it like?
It's like being Black in America with modern day experiences
While serving in a time warp in our world's historical past.

Being The Only African American

Sitting on the missionary compound porch
Sipping mint julep tea
The sins of the ancestors
Kick in
And the ingrown toe nail of master/slave

- 219 -

Chapter Forty Eight

Sneaks into the day.
My American status often gets muddied
In the rich sepia tones of the people around us.
I am often mistaken by some of our missionaries
As subservient
Because we are waited on hand and foot
At our compound by the kinship of my brown Haitian sisters and
brothers.
Its innate.
It's a non-tangible
Difficult to document.
An inkling.
An attitude.
A look.
A sharpness of tone.
An impatience.
An assumed expectation.
So I keep myself busy
Alienated in the communion
Of burying myself in the great commission;
So I won't notice my fellow American's personal exclusions and
omissions.
I challenge myself to go over and beyond
The thoughts of the melanin in my flesh
As I dance and play tag with the pink elephants in the room
As I strive and strain
in spite of the blackness and whiteness of me
to give God His best.

CHAPTER FOURTY NINE
UNGRATEFUL

God forgive me
I make such an idol of myself
I worry and worry
I whine and whine
I complain and show frustration.
The plane is late
Will I miss my connection?
Will the luggage with the medicine and food
Arrive when I arrive?
A lost passport!
God fixes it.
Upgrades my flight
My luggage arrives and is waiting for us
A friend of a friend of a friend
Who knows somebody
who knows somebody
Provides an emergency passport.
Snack for 200 kids
Multiplies to feed 317.
Yet I never, ever
spend the same amount
of gratitude energy
to match the same wattage
of my worry
of my ungraciousness
and my lack of belief.

CHAPTER FORTY NINE

My ungrateful attitude
outweighs me
Unbalanced by my meager,
"Thank God!"
That is permeated with the smell of
"It's about time!"
And I quickly become
consumed
By my next
worry,
My next
frustration
My next
complaint.

Another Spiritual Flaw

When I'm not tuned
into the Holy spirit
My American ingenuity
turns into
Missionary insensitivity.

When God When?

When God When?
When Christ's Word
Stands up off of the page
Gets their walking paper
Dewing the do of the Bible
That's when.
That's when my will
Will finally get done on earth
As it is in heaven.

CHAPTER FIFTY
DEFINING STATEMENTS

Three statements stick with me. Statements that keep me under conviction; statements that call me to accountability.

STATEMENT ONE

"Miss Yolantha, de chuldrun, dey wait for you like the desert lays in wait for the rain."

I come from a long Southern heritage of farmers. I remember, as a little girl in Eagle Lake, Texas on a once in a life time summer visit with my grandparents, sitting on the hot, sweltering porch imitating my grandmother fanning herself as we stared off into the horizon day after day waiting and watching for rain. How amazing to think of someone waiting for me with the same energy of expectation.

STATEMENT TWO

"We thought that our Black brothers and sisters in America had forgotten us. But because you come, we know that they have not forgotten. Every night Miss Yolantha, my wife and my children, we pray for you, and we thank God for you. Every night we ask God to bless all of America because of the work that you do here in Haiti."

For years I've found this statement intimidating, haunting, humbling.

To think, that I, a sinner
A woman who often harbors
Hateful secret conversations.
A women who fronts a smile

CHAPTER FIFTY

When she is secretly spitting
In the face of her accusers.
A woman who lays awake at night
Replaying conversations of the day
With the sinful game of …
"this is what I shoulda said…
This is what I shoulda done…
Next time it happens…"
Dare I think or even believe
For one moment
That an act or deed or word
That I have said or done on the mission field
Stands between America
And destruction…
Between America
And her blessings?

STATEMENT THREE

It's what I do.

One summer a young man, who had worked with me for 3 years as a translator and disciplinarian of the children couldn't come to assist me because he had other obligations for the summer. The night before we were to return to America he arrived. He had hitch hiked and walked over 43 miles to see me. I was flabbergasted and caught completely off guard. In 3 crushes and 2 marriages, never has anyone cared for me to this magnitude. All I knew to do was to hug him tightly and tell him, "Thank you for coming. It is so good to see you."

He responded, "Miss Yolantha, you have inspired me. I am very active with the children in my village, because of you."

Not knowing how to react, I hugged him again.

DEFINING STATEMENTS

"Thank you for coming, I can't believe you came all of this way to see me. How long can you stay?

"No need to thank me. I have already stayed my time." I did a quick glance at my nine, ninety nine Wal-Mart watch, barely 12 minutes had transpired.

"I must start walking back now. No need to thank me. It is what I do, Miss Yolantha, it is what I do."

Every time I get ready to prepare for another adventure in Haiti, I ask myself, "Miss Yolantha, what is it that you do?

A scripture pops into my heart and I hear a voice, "only what you do for Christ shall last."

"Marching to the beat of God's very own heart..."

WHO BETTER THAN YOU?

Truly Alive

On the mission field of Haiti
I am the hand
Touching like Jesus touched
The encouragement
Speaking like Jesus spoke
The hug comforting
Like Jesus comforted
The pat on the back
Praising like Jesus praised
The wallet
Giving like Jesus gave
The pantry
Feeding like Jesus fed.
In Haiti
My every pore exudes sunbeams of light
My soul tingles in ecstasy
My heart palpitates like an Olympic champion sprinter
My legs walk with the strength of a marathoner
Marching to the beat of God's very own heart
Breathing to the sway of God's wind
I feel the power of thunder and lightening
In the veins of my faith
A faith that not only moves mountains
But a conquering faith that straddles mountains

CHAPTER FIFTY ONE

A wise faith that prevents mountains,
A forgiving faith that erases mountains,
Now that...that is living alive.
And what a life!

Commissioned

You are all called
No one can go for you
They can go instead of you
But they can't truly be you
Going for you.

Living and Dying

No one can die for you
True Jesus, my Son died for your sins
But you still have to die
For yourself.
Will your death matter?
Will you die a dead death
Or live dead forever?

Never Underestimate The Power
Of A Black Woman's Head Rag

Time to go.
I stood in the bed of our departing truck.
The woman stood in the path.
I didn't speak her language
She didn't speak mine
We zoomed eye to eye into the depths of who we were
I thought
"There but for the grace of God go I"
I imagined she thought
"There if for the grace of God could I go."
This is where my life began to drastically change.
I'm not good at spouting off
Scriptures for every occasion
But suddenly one
Popped into my mind
"Gold and silver have I none,
But what I do have I give you."
Was that Peter's or Paul's spirit invading my body?
I untied my salvation army purchased scarf and
Extended it toward her
Her fingers flickered at her side
But she didn't budge.
I quickly hopped off of the truck
I leaned over and placed the scarf in her hand

CHAPTER FIFTY ONE

I found myself speaking the words out loud
"Gold and silver have I none
But I give you what I do have.
God's blessing and my scarf"
I could feel the impatient
Americanistic stares of the other missionaries
I turned and walked back to the truck
It was the end of my visit
I was returning to America.

A Mother's Tears

My oldest daughter wanted to do something special and memorable with me the summer before she graduated high school and before she went to college. She asked if she could come to Haiti with me. I was stunned at her request, but now at the writing of this book she has gone with me to Haiti twice in addition to taking 2 mission trips of her own.

The people fell in love with her. They absolutely adored her. Men, women, boys, girls alike. I did not have to baby sit her, she held her own. Every Christian mother should have the joy of seeing their Christian children serving God.. There is no joy that supersedes the joy of knowing that one has done something that would make God proud.

We were in Port-au-Prince and my daughter, Erin, and I had just finished her first mission trip. We had just left the mountains and we were catching a plane back to Miami. We were on the tarmac and WHAM my legs went weak, my stomach plummeted and my face began to burn with the blistering heat of tears rushing to the surface. I felt a gut bucket, primitive keening of a wail coming upon me. My flesh panicked and I felt my self grabbing for pieces of me to hold myself together.

"WHAT'S WRONG?" I panicked.

My soul screamed to the heavens, ashamed of the condition of my people of color. Ashamed that my dear sweet daughter had to witness these atrocities. Ashamed that I hadn't been able to protect her from the immense poverty and lack of medical attention and nakedness.

The Gift of Jesus then spoke. The Comforter softly whispered, who better to show her Haiti, than you, her mother?"

My soul picked itself back up off of the runway in Port-au-Prince and I headed arm in arm with my daughter back to America, our homeland.

CHAPTER FIFTY TWO
WRESTLING WITH THE ANGELS

Into The Wilderness

Have you ever
Gone into the wilderness?
Come with me to the
Dark places that
Christians don't share
Which is most unfortunate.
Jesus, Himself showed us
That the wilderness is
The place where the truest
And most real testimony hides

The Cross Thing

What is this thing called the Cross
Most of my life
I've been taught
To focus on the cross
Of rigid rejections,
The Cross of
Never ending negativity
Hurts, pains and failures.
Isn't there more to the cross?
Doesn't God also
Bless us with the cross
As a symbol of righteous resurrection
The cross as a symbol
Of everlasting joy,
The cross as a symbol of victory
And of enlightened empowerment?
I was taught
We all have a cross to bare
A cross linked with
Illness,
Skin color and gender
Lack of brain power,
Lack of beauty,
Lack of finances.
I've heard people say their one lazy eye,
Or having one foot

WRESTLING WITH ANGELS

Shorter than the other
Or their lisp or stuttering
Or wheel chair
Was their cross to bare
I grew up and centered most of my life
On the pain of Jesus' stripes
And
The hurt
Of being a Christian rather than
Recognizing them as a mechanism for
healing
Or
I just end up ignoring healing when it comes
or I just boldly bask in it
With a sense of entitlement.
When I think the Cross
Very rarely do I focus
On the walking on water,
Water to wine miracles,
Forgetting the feeding of thousands
With one little boys lunch box meal,
Forgetting the raising of the dead,
The sight given to the blind,
The ability to walk for the lame,
Ignoring all of the miraculous healings
Of this cross thing
At the cross, at the cross
Where my Savior died
Where the blood was applied
What is this thing called the cross?

CHAPTER FIFTY TWO

What Is Wrong With Me?

What's wrong with me?
God whispers that I have the same power
Available to me through my praise and the Holy Spirit
That He used in the resurrection of His son,
The same power that splashed
The vivid crimson paint on the petals of the rose,
The same passionate power of thunder,
The searing power of lightening,
Yet I sit depressed,
Rocking in my recliner,
Surrounded by miss-matched Salvation Army furniture and décor
from the Goodwill
And watch reruns of Oprah.
What is wrong with me?

Nudging

I feel the nudging of God saying,
"YOU CAN, YOU CAN, YOLANTHA"
But will I?

Stick Mentality Versus Cross Mentality

Am I carrying my cross or am I just dragging a stick?
Am I giving my all to God or
Just tossing him a stick and expecting Him
To chase it and bring it back as a mansion?
No one but God and I can honestly say
When I've given my all and
When I've done the best I can do.
It seems to operate on two plains.
One plain is my human best,
The other plain is my spiritual best.
When I manage to marry the two,
Synchronizing them,
Something phenomenal happens.
I step off into the extraordinary on the human side
And the supernatural on the spiritual side.
Whew, that's scary talk.
It's things like this that have turned me
Into a peculiar person.

Hiding From God

It is very frustrating
When a woman
Doesn't know
God's will for her life.
You flit around experimenting
With the latest religious fad.
You live in stagnation out of fear
Of doing the wrong thing, or
Fear of not being equipped enough.
You live in denial,
Out of fear of not wanting to go through the fire
In order to have all of the
'unwilling' parts of ones life
Burnished away.
You take the easy way out
Letting the will of others
Control your life
Make your decisions for you.
Perhaps you even confuse
The busy-ness of serving others
With the business of serving God.
But…but…but…
I've found that
The worst thing for me
Is knowing
God's will for my life

CHAPTER FIFTY TWO

And
My
Not
Being
Willing to do it.
It's horrid.
My conscience nags at me constantly
Attacking me at the most inopportune times
When you think you're hiding from God
Your friends expose you
Your coworkers
Your husband
Your children
Expose you.
Your bank
Your boyfriend
Expose you.
Avoiding
Or evading God
Is like trying to hide from the water
By taking refuge in the ocean.

The Children

The summer of 2006, our translator, François told me about a poor preacher who is a baker and is trying to feed some children. François gave me a letter from his friend to give to our missionary leaders. I presented the letter to the other missionaries, they quickly glanced at it and tossed it aside. So I too dismissed the letter.

The following summer of 2007, 365 days later the Mayor of the area greeted me the moment my feet landed on the mountain.

"Did anyone tell you about the children? Didn't anyone give you the letter? Did you get the letter?" He grew impatient.

I stammered out, "Yes" remembering vaguely about the letter from the year before.

"I must take you to see the children. The local baker would bake bread and at night the abandoned children would come and pick up the bread crumbs left at the market at the end of the day. The baker then tried to bake a loaf of bread for these children but when the abandoned children heard, they came from all around. There are too many children for the baker to feed. So he tries to feed them 3 times a month. "

"How many children are there?"

"Here, they are here."

We enter a room the size of my front porch about 30 feet by 12. I am overwhelmed I count approximately 76 children. Some laps are holding 2 and 3 smaller children and the children keep shifting, so 76 was the best I could do. Many of them are without clothes. I reach in my Wal-Mart back pack knowing that I don't have enough and begin to hand out crackers. But to my astonishment, God sees that every child gets fed. The back pack seemed bottomless. And then, to my human amazement, after every one had their crackers, I was able to dump out even more from the backpack for the children to have crackers again on tomorrow. I whisper a thank you that is insufficient for such a sufficient God.

"I need you to help me, help me to feed these children. They live on the mountains, abandoned, many of them naked like wild animals." the baker said.

"Where are the parents?"

"Some dead from disease, the fever, AIDs. Some have left them with family and friends while they go to the Dominican Republic to find work, never to return or be heard of again. The families and friends are too poor to take care of the extra mouths, so they are made to leave. Can you help us?"

My heart wrenched inside of me. THESE CHILDREN MUST BE FED, HAVE CLEAN WATER, BE CLOTHED, AND HAVE ACCESS TO AN EDUCATION.

Tantrum

I yelled and argued loudly with God,
"I answered as you asked in the bible."
I said, "here am I send me.
Now what am I suppose to do?
I went,
I saw,
I ministered.
Now what am I suppose to do concerning the dire need of aban-
doned children
Living on the mountain side like wild animals?
What am I suppose to do
About children going blind from pink eye?
What am I suppose to do about all of this?
In America I'm a nobody.
I can't even afford a dentist.
I'm missing 6 teeth,
2 in front are loose and ready to fall out
I am unable to heat my home properly in the winter
I've got newspaper stuck in window cracks and under doors.
I'm suppose to say, "I am rich,
My father owns the cattle on a thousand hills
And I am His daughter, His joint heir"
So God, I need to collect
On a few of those promises.
God? Are you listening to me?"
"Thank you my dearest Yolantha for going and doing."

CHAPTER FIFTY TWO

I froze in mid tantrum.

Have you ever heard God say thank you?

A calmness came over me that surpasses all understanding.

God continued,

"Thank you for going where no one else would go,

Touching folks, no one else would touch

Speaking the words no one else would speak

Kissing the unkissable

Hugging the unhuggable

Swatting flies off of dying babies.

Thank you"

"What am I suppose to do now?" I whimpered.

"I want you to tell. Tell of what you have seen and I will then bless tremendously those who bless you by blessing the children of Haiti. Thank you for going and telling it on the mountains, now I want you to go tell it FROM the mountains"

Prayer

Dear Jesus, thank you for this opportunity, please, please, please I beg of you let me pass this test. You let me see some things and now the test is what am I going to do about it? My testimony is not about money, it is about solutions. My challenge has now become GOOD WORK versus GOD'S WILL. Help me Jesus, help me. Help me pray like you

Father God, Father Daddy
Thy will be done.

But What Do You Do?

I've seen and experienced a lot in my more than 55 years,
But what do you do when you discover 76 abandoned children
Living naked, like wild animals on the mountainside?
I've rubbed elbows with 2 Heisman trophy winners
Earl Campbell and Franco Harris
I've won beauty pageants
I've seen the Rocky Mountains by the light of the full moon
Touched a stalactite in Carlsbad Cavern
I've seen the Niagara Falls thrice
But what do you do when you discover 76 abandoned children
Living like wild animals on the mountain side
I've been stuck for over an hour on the 16th floor of an elevator
I've broken my arm
I've been called the "N" word and had folks talk about my mama
I've been the victim of a murder attempt
But what do you do when you discover 76 abandoned children
Living like wild animals on the mountainside?
I've lived on food stamps and government cheese and WIC ap-
proved milk
The most I've ever had in the bank was $2000 and that was for
only about 2 weeks
I've eloped and got married in the courthouse
I've jumped on my bed and eaten cold pizza for breakfast
I've fallen asleep saying my prayers on my knees
I've had tumors removed and tested for cancer

WRESTLING WITH ANGELS

Shucks, I've ridden in a helicopter
But what do you do when you discover 76 abandoned children
Living like wild animals on the mountainside?
You run back to America and get help.

The sharing of this book is me running back to America for help. It is the testimony, rants and raves, prayers, essays, conversations and poems of a woman chosen by God (surely by Him, cause if I was doing the interviewing and hiring, knowing all that I know about me, I never would have employed me). If I were David, this book is my book of Psalms. And like David, I've written about my life with God, the joys and tribulations of a woman who desired to dare to be called a woman after God's own Heart.

"Angels watchin over me my Lord..."

CHAPTER FIFTY THREE
WHY ME?

Why me?
I'm asking, not angrily
Or in a what did I do to deserve this sort of way.
But in a humble,
God, I'm not worthy of your attention sort of way.
Why me?
I have no power
No influence,
I'm not moneyed or sugar daddy honeyed
I've got no political clout
My own personal earth poverty gets in the way
Of the providential poverty
suffered by authentically starving folks.
Why me?
I asked a stranger as I shared a testimony
about the abandoned children
Standing in the line at Wal-Mart.
The woman in front of her
Had been eavesdropping.
She leaned around the other stranger
I had been talking to and said
"God knew it would affect you
so deeply that you wouldn't be able to let it go."
The stranger,
the Angel in the Wal-Mart line was right.

CHAPTER FIFTY THREE

I sleep very well, but in the waking hours of my every day I am haunted by the eyes housed in hopeless abandonment on the mountainsides of Haiti.

Living the death of waiting, waiting, waiting…

I can't let it go.

Making a Difference

Everything
I
Learned about
the real
Me
I
Learned on
the mission field.

What Is The Mission Field?

The mission field is an awesome place
Which presents awesome situations
That yield awesome testimonies.
It is right across the ocean or
It's sitting or even sleeping right next to you
It's the Master's program for faith
It's the testing ground by which testimonies are made
It's the making or breaking point of religion
It's the Christ of the Christian
Or the evil of the Devil
It's turning Sodom and Gomorrah into glory land
Or it's just business as usual
Waiting for the next missionary to take a stand.

Why Me

Now I Lay Me Down To Sleep

I thank you without rhyme or reason
Because you bless me when I'm in and out of season
I thank you and praise you for who you are.
The Almighty
The God of Glory
The God of Wealth and Provisions
The God of Miracles
The God of I can't but He can
The God of Approachability
The God of Love, Peace and Value and Worthiness
The God of Details
I thank you for the $10 crumpled under the sofa cushion
When I thought I was broke
I thank you for the $100 somebody snuck into my purse at
church
I thank you for the two dollars donated by the first grader
Michaela
What a sacrifice of her allowance she has made
I thank you and I thank you and I thank you
God I thank you for my family,
God bless Erin,
God bless Diamond,
God bless Mother, and Daddy,
God bless my 4 brothers
Raphael, Thaxter, Xerxes and Burdick,
Amen

"What difference can I make?
Who do I think I am?"

CHAPTER FIFTY FOUR
MOSES AND THE BURNING BUSH

The Christmas Tree

On my way to home visits
Today I struggled
My homesickness strangled me
Today I served
A hundred and eighty something starving kids at VBS
What difference can I make?
Who do I think I am?
God, forgive me for presuming!
The heat was intense in my nostrils
I breathed it in
Thick like hot molasses
The pain of the uphill climb
Was finally beginning to psyche me out
My age was ringing its toll
"one foot in front of the other,
One foot in front of the other"
I chanted over and over
I rounded the path wearing a back pack
Loaded with beans, rice, toothpaste, toothbrushes
Miniature hotel soaps, miniature shampoos and lotions
A long strapped purse draped over one shoulder
Full of baby clothes,
I strained barely keeping another pouch
2 inches off the ground

CHAPTER FIFTY FOUR

Full of girly-girl things
I painstakingly rounded the end of the old rugged road
The site slapped me in the face
A site that threw me onto the knees of my heart
A bush adorned
Like a Christmas tree
Fully adorned with foam Crosses
The crosses the children made in Vacation Bible School this
morning
Surely the burning bush of Moses burned as bright as this.

Ocean Spit

I have nothing to my name
Except a van
2 televisions
A lawnmower and a piano
And 2 daughters.
No savings
No retirement
No traditional job
No insurance
No benefits
But the call came...
"WHOM SHALL I SEND?
I answered
SEND ME.
It's like spitting in the ocean,
What difference am I making
Against the helplessness
Of extreme poverty
To a nation
From a place in a nation
Where I have no clout
No personal economic power
Yet to the children of Haiti
I am an American
I am their color
And to them, I am rich

CHAPTER FIFTY FOUR

To the village children
I smell of hope
Something in my
Journey as an American
Something
In my battles with racism and bigotry and welfare
As an American
Something
In my years of horrendous domestic abuse
As an American
Gives compassion to my passion
So I spit and I spit and I spit
Into the ocean
Til' I'm dry
Then I suck on the inside of my jaws
And I spit again
Because I not only comprehend
I understand.

Sweet Smelling Sacrifice

R eading through one of my past blue books I discovered a scripture reference. I had scrawled Philippians 4:10-20. This scripture validated one of God's earlier promises to me in America during my earlier personal turmoils of domestic violence, joblessness, poverty and evictions. The 17th verse states that Paul is most appreciative of the consistency of love and gifts from the church of Philippi. But Paul expresses that he is even more excited over "the well earned reward you will have because of your kindness...they are like a sweet smelling sacrifice that pleases God well. And it is He who will supply all your needs from His riches in glory." (Living Bible paraphrased) In this joy I have a sisterhood with Paul, because something inside me glows for the kingdom gifts waiting for those who encourage and support me in God's calling on my life on behalf of the children of Haiti. There will be an asterisk in each of their lives come judgment day that says "and because you did 'this' for Yolantha I shall bless you with..." (Living Bible paraphrased) To me, like to Paul...that is awesome.

"Holy cows in the pasture."

WOMAN SHALL NOT LIVE BY BREAD ALONE

Man Shall Not Live by Bread Alone

What does that really, really, really mean?
As a child that meant, I had to eat my vegetables
and my liver and drink my milk
As I matured I asked
What should the rest of the buffet consist of?
I knew the rest of the scripture said, "but on the word of God."
For most new Christians that phrase is
Puzzling, spiritual -psychobabble.
This is where I was in dire need of discipleship.
This is where American Christians
Are destitute in fulfilling the Great Commission.

It says, go ye therefore, and teach all nations, baptizing them in the name of the Father, and of the Son and of the Holy Ghost: teaching them to observe all things whatsoever I have commanded you: and, lo, I am with you always, even unto the end of the world. Amen.

It's the "teaching them" part that very rarely gets done
As a new Christian
I filled my plate with family, and lived on church going,
And the do-gooders way of life.
I became religiously obese,

CHAPTER FIFTY FIVE

Which left me spiritually out of shape and
Lethargic with a spiritual loneliness;
I became feverishly impatient with folks less religious than I
I became flabby with flippant holier than thou-ness.

Together We Eat

I t is one thing to give money for food or to even deliver the food. But the real question becomes,
"WILL YOU EAT WITH ME?"

For 2 years I had been feeding the children a snack upon arrival in the mornings and then a snack at the end of our day. One day my dear friend and fellow missionary Cissy came real close to me, unwrapped a cracker and demanded, "Eat!!!"

"But, but, but…" I protested. "If I eat, some child won't have anything."

"The children have never seen you eat. Eat with them!"

I looked at the emaciated children staring at me as they ate in a state of euphoria. I took a bite of the orange peanut buttery cracker. The children froze in mid-chew, the whole room suddenly broke into a smile as the children nodded their heads in approval as if to say, "Together we eat."

Man shall not live by bread alone,
Man shall not eat
All by himself in solitude…
But by breaking bread…
With each other…
Together

CHAPTER FIFTY FIVE

Thank You Cynthia

Cynthia is part of my wonderful support group through Sunday School class. We call our class, Women of Faith. They provide me prayer, financial, spiritual and moral support. I can lay my soul out vulnerable before them and they help paste me back together with spiritual glue.

One summer Cynthia snuggled up close into my personal space and gave me a piece of fabric and a piece of lace like trimming.

"Trade it for something instead of spending money for everything," she suggested.

Later when I was packing I tucked the fabric and trim into a pocket of my denim travel skirt and I didn't think about it again til I'd been in Haiti for a couple of days. This particular day, I came upon a Haitian woman sitting beside the road, embroidering a table cloth. I inadvertently stuck my hands in my pockets and discovered the items Cynthia had given me. I walked up to the Haitian woman, fingered her magnificent work and since I don't speak Creole I made positive American sounds of beauty. I gave her the fabric and trim bestowed upon me by Cynthia and walked away

"Miss, Miss, Miss…"

I turned. She hugged the gift of fabric to her bosom and rocked back and forth. I waved, turned back around and whispered, "Thank you Cynthia." From this point on I vowed to always, bring needles, embroidery thread and pieces of remnant fabric with me on the mission field. "Yes, thank you Cynthia," Woman cannot live by bread alone but by "every word that proceeded out of the mouth of God.

WOMAN SHALL NOT LIVE BY BREAD ALONE

Thank you for teaching me that living is doing the Word of God and
that all of my doings should be living the words of God.

I'm finally learning
The operative word is LIVE…
Not sustaining breath living
Not brain cell living,
Not heart beat living, but by
The LIVING of God's Word…
It is the doing of God's Word that
Makes authentic life happen.

"Feed my lambs..."

CHAPTER FIFTY SIX
THE JUMP ROPE

Every time a missionary passed by the little girl would grab at her tummy and rub, indicating that she was hungry. One morning, on my way to breakfast, the child blocked my path and rubbed her tummy furiously. I heaped extra eggs, cheese, mango and oatmeal on my plate and sat out on the porch. I fed my hungry friend with the same joy and satisfaction with which my mother fed me as a child. After the last bite she hugged me and scurried off.

Ten minutes later, another missionary approached. My little breakfast buddy blocked her path and made the same grab at her stomach, begging with pleading eyes.

"Oh you poor thing, come let me feed you. You are hungry."

I was stupefied. "Why the little con artist."

My accusation was confirmed when within 30 more minutes she had another missionary by the pity of his heart, emptying his pocket of granola bars and peppermints to feed the 'poor hungry child'.

Later, on my way to lunch, after a rousing morning of Vacation Bible School with an attendance of a little over 300 children, a small hand snuck itself into mine. It was the little hungry girl smiling expectantly up at me, rubbing her tummy. My inner city self kicked in. I humped my shoulders, bent my arms at the elbow, with my hands palm up and shook my head. "No."

She removed her hand from mine and skipped over to another missionary who took pity and brought the child a heaping plate of food. The suckered missionary and I sat on the porch and watched her eat. Barely half an hour later the little darling was snuggled up to another unsuspecting missionary leaning on her missionary bosom eating from the missionary's plate.

Hardly an hour and 3 plates of food later, the little hungry girl plopped down beside me as I read from my Bible on the porch. She rubbed her tummy.

It hit me like a ton of bricks. It wasn't food she was begging for. It was attention. It was a need to be noticed and valued. Food was not enough; would never be enough. The full meaning of Mathew 4:4 splashed over me as if someone had dumped me with a mop bucket full of ice water. Man shall not live by bread alone. This child was dead inside, empty inside, emaciated for want of being validated. I placed my Bible in her lap and went to my luggage to search for something sustaining to give her.

As I searched my luggage, my mind churned. Some how I knew that even if I could speak her language, just reading from the Bible would not be enough either. As sacrilegious as that sounds I was now facing a crucial moment of truth and turning point for my life. The fullness of Matthew 4:4 says that "It is written, MAN SHALL NOT LIVE ON BREAD ALONE, BUT ON EVERY WORD THAT PROCEEDS OUT OF THE MOUTH OF GOD".

Reading the Bible is not enough. I know, I've read the bible. To LIVE ON something is to be motivated by; spurred into action by that something. What am I living on? Granted studying scripture passed the time, calmed me down upon occasion, and gave me some insights into trying circumstances. However; today my revelation was that there is an action component missing. Something that some-how over the years I missed. Something that is the pure essence of righteousness. The whole trap of apathetic living, self pity, the syndrome of "is this all there is", joylessness, blowing with the wind… perhaps comes from relying on man's bread, man's ingredients, living on man's latest motivational recipes and self help books…and not from LIVING ON the nurturing dependency of the life sustaining, action wielding manna from heaven.

In the span of 2 years I had read and studied, THE PRAYER OF JABEZ, PURPOSE DRIVEN LIFE, THE HEAVENLY MAN, WOMEN WHO WIN, DRIVEN BY ETERNITY, END OF THE SPEAR, THE ONE YEAR BIBLE, GOD'S PROMISES, REVOLU-TION-THE RADICAL CHRISTIAN, MASTERLIFE, THE EDGE OF GLORY, GOD'S TRANSFORMING WORD, A JOURNEY IN FAITH, THE UTMOST FOR HIS HIGHEST.

Yet, I found myself hiding in the consuming time of studying rather than being consumed by actions spurred on by my studies. I was finding that knowledge is docile, stagnant, petrified. I was becoming a junkie to reading books. I would feel a depression coming over me as I read, dreading my approach to the last page as it crept chapter by chapter toward me. I became anxious for my next book fix. I have to admit I was gaining lots of knowledge, but one evening after I finished reading THE UTMOST FOR HIS HIGHEST for the second time, that still small voice that sneaks up on you in the middle of the night, pricked my heart.

"Okay when are you going to stop hiding behind reading and begin living a life that others can read?

But that wasn't even enough of a kick in my spiritual behind. I am an avid journal keeper. I've kept some form of a journal since 1988. The voice continued.

"And by the way when are you going to stop journaling and live the journey?"

How humbling.

Aha! There it was. One lonely jump rope wrapped tightly in the side pocket of my carry on luggage. I took the rope to the little girl, only to discover she had no clue how to use it. Matthew 4:4 came alive as I clumsily taught her to do something I had not done in over 40 years. As we laughed and giggled and stumbled and tripped over our awkwardness...BUT ON EVERY WORD THAT PROCEEDS OUT OF THE MOUTH OF GOD...took on a new meaning.

This scripture had nothing to do with knowing or memorizing scripture. I learned that "living the Word" meant "jumping, laughing, tripping, giggling the Word." Supper time came, the little girl begged no one for food. Instead she went about impressing the missionaries with her newly found skill of jumping rope.

The next morning as I ate my breakfast, the little girl stood beside me smiling and methodically jumping rope, her plate of food I'd prepared for her barely touched.

"Yup, tis true even little girls do not live by bread alone".

COUNT

I t was the start of the last day. We always offer the children the Plan of Salvation on that final part of our journey. On this particular visit we culminated by asking any children who wanted to accept Jesus as their personal Lord and Savior to come and kneel with me. I whispered to the missionary standing beside me to count the number of children coming. He began to count, then stopped.

"It's about 50."

"Count to see how many."

He began to count them again. "It's about 55 or 60."

"Count them," I hissed.

"Just say there are 70 of them." The other missionary huffed.

I got up off of my knees, got in his face. "I said count them! Fifty, fifty-five, sixty, seventy, those are man's numbers. Don't round off these children." I raised my voice, "COUNT THEM!!! I WANT GOD'S COUNT!!!"

The missionary turned, American style, and walked away from me. So I counted God's children for myself. God's number was 89. Not 50, 55 or 60 or 70...but eighty nine. What's the big deal? Even if I just say there are around 70 children, what if you or I were part of the 19 not counted. Those 19 matter to God, so those 19 matter to me. Not 50, not 55, not 60, not 70...but 89.

God's Children

Many of the children are walking 12 miles to see the missionary
The odd Black woman from America.
Everywhere I went the second year
I drew a crowd and the children yelled for me
From across the fields
Shouting who-hooooooooo
I echoed back who-hooooooooooo
Mix Youlanda, do you remember me? How about me? You re-
member me?
Mix youlaaaaaaaanda
You are welcome
Left over from last year
Jumping out suddenly in front of me
The deep earth toned body sings
With a huge Cheshire cat smile and a thick Creole accent
"Yes Geezuz luhs me"

COUNT

How Do You Know That?

I was sitting with the rest of the missionaries when I noticed the pastor of the church standing in the doorway trying to get my attention. The whole church was watching. He was waving his hand toward me as if to say come here. I almost did the thing I forever fuss at my students in America for. I caught myself wanting to look behind me as if the person talking to me is perhaps talking to the person behind me. For fear of appearing disrespectful or looking stupid I pointed to myself.

"Who me?"

"Yes." Nodded the Pastor. I walked across the front of the church with everyone watching me.

What in the world could the pastor want that he would come out of the pulpit and whisk me away from the safety net of the other missionaries. I begin to sweat big time. I didn't even have a translator. I followed the Pastor into a room and was overwhelmed by a room full to the brim with children overlapping each others laps, and standing sideways in order for everyone to fit. Children were 3 and 4 deep all the way around the room. The Pastor smiled real big and left.

"Oh my God."

I almost hyperventilated. I didn't (and I'm ashamed to say still do not) speak a word of Creole. An adult female voice spoke with excitement and animation.

"Let me tell you my favorite story in the Old Testament. It's the story of Miriam. Now can anyone tell me who Miriam was?"

I breathed a huge sigh of relief. I had some help. This woman spoke perfect English. Then I realized that the excited and animated voice was mine. (aaaahhh fiddlesticks, what am I thinking? How do I get out of this pickle?)

"I will translate for you!" Out of the clear blue sky a teenager that I didn't recognize began boldly imitating me and translating what I had said to the children in Creole. He imitated me perfectly just like François, my seasoned translator and friend.   One hand shot up in the air, waving back and forth furiously.

"Yes?" I said, looking at the excited child, "Tell us. Who is Miriam?"

I figured the young boy was gonna say something off topic, because even in America the majority of the children have no clue who Miriam was.

"Miriam is Moses sistah" the young boy proudly exploded.

Surprised, I grinned and clapped, "Who hooooo, very, very good."

"Who-whoooooo" imitated all of the children.

"How do you know that? How do you know who Miriam is?"

"Ah, Miss Yolantha," he cooed in perfect Creole English, "You taught me dat last year. When you taught us dat God can use even me. Dat's how I now dat!!!"

I was silent for a moment, then began to tell the story of Moses, Miriam's brother.

Yea, I humbly thought, God can use even me...a 55 something, Kentuckian by way of Indiana, Missouri and Texas, spouse abuse survivor, unemployed mother of 2.

PLANTING YOUR OWN BLESSING

My spirit is vexed, unsettled
Nothing I can put my finger on
No one thing or persons fault
My ageless sins and doubts are upon me
Something is wrestling me
Tangling me up with powerful invisible gossamer threads
Yet nothing I can speak about
Ask about or
Tell about
Its like when you walk through an invisible spider web
And try to pull it off of your face
And can't quite get a grip of it
If I cry people will ask why am I crying
And I'll have to say I don't know
Is it the overwhelming poverty
The overwhelming lack
The overwhelming hopelessness
The overwhelming realities
The other missionaries don't speak about it
They laugh and talk and look overly loud
But maybe it just seems loud
When we leave the shores of America
Compared to the quietness of
Lack, hoplessnessness and high infant mortality statistics.
Out of the corner of my eye I see something bright
Moving down the path

There are 2 of them

A mother and a daughter, as they get closer

I see they are wearing a bright scarf, my scarf from the past

Walking down the path

Twice

It has been torn in half so God could bless

A mother and her daughter

Through the power of one scarf

They both saw me and waved real big

My spirit popped like super man ripping off his

Clark Kent disguise and my non tangible self seemed to fly into

the air

God used a seed I planted 3 years earlier

To feed me in my missionary hour of need

A peace began hugging my heart,

I felt my spirit beginning to settle.

CHAPTER FIFTY NINE
RELIGIOUS RACISM

My Seventh Day Adventists Sabbath Experience

We are meticulously cared for except for on Saturdays, by Mother Ivy an eighty something, die hard, 7th Day Adventist. She's the kind of non-compromising traditionalist that causes the eyes of my staunch fellow Southern Baptists in America to glaze over because of her many rules, rituals, regulations and her devotion to our Saturdays as her Sabbath.

Madame Ivy, founder of our mission work
I eat from your table
Food prepared by your hands
On legs that have never tasted pants
What God do you serve to make you
Such an inspirational and mighty woman?
The other missionaries spit out the words
Seven Day Adventist with raised brow undertones.
Yet the Holy Spirit in me says
If I am good enough to eat your food and sleep in your beds
Then I am good enough to go to church with you.
Oh what I found
Same Bible
Same God.
Same Jesus
Then something strange happened

The people stood up
Church, I thought was over.
As we exited, some of the adults received a rock.
Mother Ivy took one and gave it to me.
Then took one of her own
I followed her into the next building.
We sat down
Someone prayed in Creole
An usher took my rock
Which I discovered was used as a counting system
Then Mother Ivy got up, walked away, leaving me sitting.
She came back with a white metallic bowl
Like my grandmother used to use to shell and snap beans in
Mother Ivy bent down, slipped off my shoes
And began washing my feet.
My soul leapt inside of me like Peter
"Noooooo I can't have you wash my feet"
I'm not worthy to have this saint
This Mother Teresa like figure wash my feet.
She continued, so gently anointing me for service
She like Jesus was loving me not as a religion
But as a person.
Mother Ivy, her task complete
Sat down.
Oh Jesus help me
My hands trembled
It was my turn to wash hers.

It's Hard

"**M**other Ivy, how did the mission get started?"
Mrs. Ivy is my Mother Theresa of Haiti. Her life has been absolutely amazing yet her humbleness, as befitting any saint, makes it difficult to gather all of the details. In addition her folk hero status within the village community often times leads to a myriad of embellishments about the life of our living folk hero. What little of the story I have has been pieced together, here and there down through the 10 years of my work on the mission field as one of the first African American female missionaries to the impoverished remote mountain village of Ranquitte-Calhoun Spady, Haiti. Mother Ivy, twice a widow, is now way into her eighties, becoming arthritic and is extremely hard of hearing. This also makes gleaning her story a challenge because at any moment, with a furrowed brow, she may announce, "WHAT? WHAT? I CAN'T HEAR YOU, I'M GETTING OLD!", abruptly ending ones audience with her by fanning though the air with her well worn saintly hands. One year to all of the other missionary's amazement she let me interview her. She told bits of her story.

"My first husband disappeared one night many years ago, 'they' came and got him and killed him. My sister and I escaped to America for a while. I went to nursing school and when it was safe for me I returned home to Haiti. I would sit here on my porch. And I got tired of seeing the tiny coffins of children paraded by my house as baby after baby died in the village. I couldn't just sit idly by and watch. But what could I do?

CHAPTER FIFTY NINE

Mother Ivy searched my face as if I had the answer; then she continued.

"I invited some of the new mothers to my home and taught them a little of what I learned in America about nutrition. I showed them how to cook beans and rice to keep the babies alive. There were fewer coffins going by, but before long as the babies became toddlers, the young mothers didn't know how to watch and protect them from the open fire. It is hard here. Some times the children would be so hungry that they would reach in the fire for the food and receive severe burns. That's how I was discovered. I had gone into the city to buy gauze and medicine for a child who had been burned badly. Some Americans on holiday in Haiti were told to come meet me. Someone had shared with them about the work I was doing up in the mountains. They took pity on me and my children and went back and told their friends in America and that's how it all got started."

"Mother Ivy, what is your greatest accomplishment and your biggest challenge here in Haiti?"

"WHAT? WHAT? Miss Yolantha speak up I am old I can't understand you."

I raised my voice like I used to when I spoke to my 100 year old grandmother when I was younger. "WHAT'S THE BEST THING AND THE WORST THING THAT HAS HAPPENED TO YOU?" I shouted as respectfully as I could.

"The thing I am most proud of is that I have started a sewing class where the women are learning to make things that they can sell in order to support their families. But we have no electricity so we need foot pedal sewing machines. They are so expensive. They cost any where from 250 to 350 U.S. dollars in the city."

Mother Ivy continues in the same breath, "The lowest point?" Some years ago a little boy came up missing. The parents couldn't find him anywhere. The whole village was out searching for the child. A few weeks passed and the child was found."

She looked deep into my eyes. "Some people in another village had roasted him and eaten him. It is hard here Miss Yolantha. Very hard."

Leaving Day

It was leaving day. Oodles of children chased after our truck. We drove away sparking up dust from the parched roads. One by one the little children dropped away except for one ebony bronzed boy, running with the determination of an Olympic champion.

The little boy ran reaching for me shouting, "goodbye teechuh, good bye teechuh! I reached for him as the truck began to increase speed. He jumped up and high fived my hand. "yes Jesus loves me." he grinned up, running, huffing and puffing. Bobo America, Bobo!!! bobo America, Bobo!!!"

Our engines sped along leaving the little boy with his nakedness as he grew smaller and smaller along the horizon. Our truck drew further and further away. I was silent for the 12 mile ride to the airport in Pignon. Upon arrival at the airport, I could still feel the sting of the running boy's hand in mine. When I finally reclaimed my heart I asked one of the translators, "What did the little boy mean when he shouted at me "bobo, America, bobo!!!""

The translator leaned in real close to me and said, "the little boy was telling you, "KISS AMERICA, KISS!"

"Pick a day, any day..."

CHAPTER SIXTY
HOPE

Back in America I began telling everybody about "the children". I began getting advice from other missionaries in Haiti who had built orphanages and were doing what I am needing to do. One person advised me to find a lawyer in my church and get him or her to walk me through the process of becoming a non-profit organization. This person also suggested that perhaps the lawyer under the circumstances would donate his services and maybe someone from my church would help cover the fee of incorporating.

Another missionary I called suggested, "Yolantha, start out finding a way to get finances to feed the children once a week."

"Once a week? I exploded.

"Yes, that will give the children hope."

"Hope?" My voice level elevated several more notches. "HOW IS THAT HOPE?" I blew out a spurt of dragon like air. "My daughters eat 3 times a day and all in between if they so desire."

The missionary on the other end of the line gently laughed which immediately annoyed me.

"Remember the children are not eating every day any way. And if they know that they will eat, let's just say…every Wednesday. They will have hope starting on Sunday. They know that in 3 days they will eat. On Monday they are full of hope because they know that in 2 days they will eat. On Tuesday they will be full of joy because they know in one day, tomorrow, they will eat. On Wednesday their hope is fulfilled, because on Wednesday they eat. On Thursday they are full of joy because on yesterday they ate. On Friday they rejoice because 2 days ago they ate. On Saturday they remember that 3 days ago, they ate. On Sunday once again they know that in 3 more days, they will eat. That is hope, Yolantha.

There was silence on the phone. I realized it was my turn to say something.

"Thank you." I said. I hung up, and like Jesus I wept.

www.ingramcontent.com/pod-product-compliance
Lightning Source LLC
Chambersburg PA
CBHW021044090426
42738CB00006B/181